LANGUAGE AND LITERACY SERIES

Dorothy S. Strickland and Celia Genishi

SERIES EDITORS

The Complete Theory-to-Practice Handbook of Adult Literacy:
Curriculum Design and Teaching Approaches
*Rena Soifer, Martha E. Irwin, Barbara M. Crumrine,
Emo Honzaki, Blair K. Simmons, and Deborah L. Young*

Literacy for a Diverse Society:
Perspectives, Practices, and Policies
Elfrieda H. Hiebert, Editor

The Child's Developing Sense of Theme:
Responses to Literature
Susan S. Lehr

The Triumph of Literature / The Fate of Literacy:
English in the Secondary School Curriculum
John Willinsky

The Child as Critic: Teaching Literature in
Elementary and Middle Schools, THIRD EDITION
Glenna Davis Sloan

Process Reading and Writing: A Literature-Based Approach
*Joan T. Feeley, Dorothy S. Strickland,
and Shelley B. Wepner, Editors*

Inside/Outside: Teacher Research and Knowledge
Marilyn Cochran-Smith and Susan L. Lytle

Literacy Events in a Community of Young Writers
Yetta M. Goodman and Sandra Wilde

The Politics of Workplace Literacy: A Case Study
Sheryl Greenwood Gowen

Whole Language Plus: Essays on Literacy
in the United States and New Zealand
Courtney B. Cazden

The Politics of Workplace Literacy

A CASE STUDY

Sheryl Greenwood Gowen

Teachers College, Columbia University
New York and London

For My Family

My mother, Jonnie Greenwood, my husband, Bill,

and my children, Jessica, Claire, and John

Published by Teachers College Press, 1234 Amsterdam Avenue
New York, NY 10027

Library of Congress Cataloging-in-Publication Data

Gowen, Sheryl Greenwood.
  The politics of workplace literacy : a case study / Sheryl Greenwood Gowen.
      p.   cm. — (Language and literacy series)
  Includes bibliographical references and index.
  ISBN 0-8077-3214-1 (alk. paper). — ISBN 0-8077-3213-3 (pbk. : alk. paper)
  1. Career development — Case studies.   2. Blue collar workers — Education — Case studies.   3. Functional literacy — Case studies.
4. Employee assistance programs — Case studies.   I. Title.
II. Series: Language and literacy series (New York, N.Y.)
HF5549.5.C35G68   1992
331.25 — dc20   92-31876

Printed on acid-free paper

Manufactured in the United States of America

99 98 97 96 95 94 93 92   8 7 6 5 4 3 2 1

You hold no stock in the prefab, purchased-pattern quilt. You do not understand the point of stitching without your heart-involvement. Without your ideas incorporated into the work, it is just an exercise, something to fill up the long evening spent without companionship.

W. Otto, *How to Make an American Quilt*

Contents

Acknowledgments

Writing a book is the process of bringing other voices, other stories, and other thoughts together to fashion them anew. This project has been no exception. Those women and men whose stories shape this book are those to whom I owe the greatest thanks, and they are the very ones whose names I cannot mention. But they know who they are, and I hope they will feel some sense of reward that their stories are being heard by others.

I could not have written this book without their help and without the support and encouragement of a wide range of colleagues and friends. Any flaws in fact or interpretation, of course, are my own responsibility.

D. Scott Enright introduced me to ethnography and gave me a vision of the research I might do for this book. His energy and good humor were an inspiration. He was an extraordinary teacher. George Jensen and Robert Probst initially encouraged me to think of publishing the study. Their confidence in the work and in my ability to write about it formed the core of endurance needed to bring such a project to fruition. I also survived on the gifts of professional interest, constructive criticism, and personal kindness from Hal Beder, Joan Carson, Joan Elifson, Hannah Fingeret, Carole Hill, Marsha Houston, Glenda Hull, Susan Lytle, Bob Probst, Mike Rose, Jacqueline Jones Royster, Jacqueline Saindon, Tony Sarmiento, Rena Soifer, Marti Singer, Sondra Stein, and Tom Valentine. Katharine Stone's willingness to read and comment on parts of the manuscript were invaluable. Rhonda Webb and Suzanne Womack were essential in their cheerful willingness to proofread, edit, and make just "one more" trip to the library. Joanne Nurss's support and wise counsel from the beginning through to the end of this project have sustained me in the face of the most difficult situations.

Shirley Brice Heath's work has shaped this project more than any other. Her genuine respect for people, her ability to recognize and celebrate their literacies, and her skill in writing about them with such grace are models of professional and personal accomplishment.

My colleagues in ethnography—Mary Ball, Barbara Fasse, Alice Gertzman, Norma Harris, Mary Jane Nations, Wendy Newstedder—have provided intellectual challenge, emotional support, and terrific fun over these past four years. This is not a process to undertake alone. I could not have asked for better companions. My dear friend Kent Leslie has been a constant balance point, generous neighbor, and surrogate parent when needed.

The editors at Teachers College Press have been a delight to work with—Sarah Biondello, Melissa Mashburn, and Faye Zucker have given me encouragement, sensible advice, and the necessary prodding I've often needed.

Finally I must thank my family, although I can never repay the sacrifices they have made for me to complete this work. My mother has been an unending source of help and support for all of us—from the dinners cooked, to the laundry folded, to the baseball games watched. My husband has endured this process with an uncommon amount of help and good spirit. And my children have been and continue to be a source of deep pleasure and surprise—Jessica for her strength and dignity, Claire for her humor and balance, and John for his energy and charm.

From this process I have learned that work is not something one carries out alone—rather it is pieced together with professional colleagues, friends, and family into a quilt of many shapes and colors, displaying a special story. Each person mentioned above, and many others left unnamed, deserves a special thanks—without their contributions, this book would never have been written.

Prologue

Out on the bay it is morning. The grind of the cicada fills silvery marshes as shrimp boats wing slowly out to drag the sea. But downtown it is still dark — a grey squeeze of buildings marking the sky. The faint whine of an ambulance echoes down streets strung with headlights prowling for spaces to park. Two blocks west of the courthouse a knot of red brick rises, inviting the sick and poor and homeless to rest, to be cared for, to be patched up, to be born, or to die.

King Memorial Hospital has been a landmark in this delta town longer than most folks can remember. Supported primarily by local tax money, it is the largest public health care facility in the area. And because of its central location, it provides employment for many of the city's residents, most of whom are women and men of color. Their work at the hospital consists primarily of cooking, cleaning, and washing — the work of their people for generations, since the slave ships brought them here three centuries ago.

Mostly they like working at "the Kings." Their coworkers are nice and the benefits are good, but they wish for better salaries, more respect, and time off on the weekends for family and church. Although a few have advanced, others have been in the same job for as long as 20 years. Many of them were born in this hospital, or their children were. They expect they will probably die here, too. Some of their children or grandchildren already have. If you ask them, they will tell you their stories: where they came from, what their lives are like, what their dreams are.

Employees at King Memorial Hospital wrote the following stories at the beginning of a workplace literacy program. They have been edited only to change identifying details. The names of all persons — workers, teachers, program planners, consultants, and tutors — who participated in this study as well as the names and details about specific institutions and locations have also been changed to protect individual and collective privacy.

1

STORY 1

I was born April 25, 1936 to a proud father (age 19) and a young mother (age 14) in the old Kings "colored hospital." The same building is used by the Medical College today. I also have three brothers, and one sister. I'm the oldest.

I completed school in 1956 (12th grade). Graduated on a Friday, and three days later, on a Monday, I was on a bus, headed to Fort Jackson Army Base, South Carolina for eight weeks basic training. I served six years in the Army Signal Corps in Pole Line Construction, and as a switchboard operator. Thanks to Uncle Sam, I got to travel to other countries like Korea, Japan, & South America. Of all the things I learn in the military, theres one thing that has helped me the most—Discipline.

After Army duty, I've held a odd assortment of jobs. Stock clerk, supervisor over 30 or more women in a shirt trimming company. We had to go out of business, because of foreign competition. I was with the shirt company for 15 years. After I lost this job, I got a job at King Memorial. Working in Housekeeping. I've worked here for four years.

I've been proposed to quite a few times. So far I'm still single and free! (smile) I've admired a lot of men, and women but I've never wanted to be "just like them." I'm unique. Like the song Miss Lena Horne did in the Wiz, "Believe in Yourself." I do, if not fully.

My hobbies are photography, drawing, & painting, when the mood hit me. Lately that ain't been too often.

STORY 2

I work at King Memorial Hospital. In the Housekeeping Department. I am 31 years old. Also I am from Bayside. I live here all my life. I come from a family of eight children. I have five sister and three brother. Also I have a daughter name La Shaundra that I love very much. She is seven years old. She give me joy and happiness. She give me support that I need in my life. Now I tell you about my job. I like my job but it's a hard working job. But people today is not the same. On the job, they treat you like you are a child and talk to you any kind of way. But I just look over them and pray for them all. But I am looking from something better out of life. One day my dream will come true. That's to be a E.K.G. That's my gold.

STORY 3

My name is Mattie Kelly and I was born in Bayside. I attended school here until I entered the 11th grade and dropped out. Worst thing I ever did. Married at the age of 19 and 2 years later started a family and been on a hard road ever since. At one time I began to think all the woe's and troubles in the world belonged to me. I even thought about killing myself, but then I would look at my girls and gain new strength. I'm glad I stuck around. I'm proud of all three. The really hard thing I had to do was get into the job market at such a late time in my life. I was 41 when I joined it before then I did jewelry home shows, but I enjoyed my job. I looked forward to getting up every morning going to work and bringing home a real paycheck even if it wasn't a lot, but then came the injury to my hand and things got hard. Sometimes the pain is unbearable but you have to keep moving and people the department heads think it nothings wrong with it and all the washers say it should be me but they don't know I'd give anything to have their good hands. I liked doing beds.

STORY 4

My name is Betty Roberts. I was born and raised in Georgia. I moved to Bayside on June 19th, 1985. I have a daughter and granddaughter there names are Janice and Natassia. When I came to Bayside I thought I wanted to be an assistant manager in a convenience store but that didn't work out. So now I am concentrating on my G.E.D. so I can farther my education. I would like to take classes to learn to be a physical therapist, because I like helping people and there families through hard times. I fill I'm a very lucky person to have a chance to work at King Memorial which is a start an opportunity to advance and better my career in the medical field.

The Goals of the Study

The stories of the men and women who wrote these narratives are the central focus of this book. Although workplace literacy has become a national issue with a glut of publications warning about the problem and proposing a variety of solutions, little has been written from the point of view of the employees involved in such programs. It is the intention of this study to consider workplace literacy from the perspective of the men and women who are defined in the public discourse as workers with inadequate literacy skills.

The themes raised in the preceding stories ground this description of how a workplace literacy project becomes a part of these writers' daily lives for nine months, how it changes or does not change them, how it meets or fails to meet their needs, and ultimately what these men and women can teach those of us who define ourselves as educators. But first, in order to give full voice to these stories and to situate my interpretations of them, the reader must also consider the broader contexts in which they (and I) are positioned. To place this study in such a frame, I provide another set of stories in Chapter 1, some perhaps more familiar to teachers and program planners.

CHAPTER 1

Literacy and the Other

I grew up in a sleepy Florida town in the 1950s. As a child, I spent much of my time swimming and fishing in the stunningly clear waters of Cape Canaveral Bay. After sixth grade, I attended the new junior high school named after General Robert E. Lee. We were the "Rebels." The young girls in the flag corps wore hats styled after those of rebel soldiers and twirled close replicas of Confederate flags. I sometimes heard the Civil War jokingly referred to as "the War of the Yankee Aggression." A strong identification with Southern history created a web of meaning that informed the everyday life of my community.

My memories of ninth grade are punctuated by the clear vision of a rocket launch from Cape Canaveral (where we were no longer allowed to play). Excused from science class, we stood on the upstairs balcony of our gleaming new school to watch John Glenn blast off into the sky. At the time it seemed exciting to be growing up in the midst of the space race. There was the cold war and the bomb, of course, but there was also Teflon and Tang, all results of the new technology.

In high school, I learned to protect myself from the threat of communism in a so-called communications course. We read J. Edgar Hoover's *The Masters of Deceit* (1958) and tried to think about what life would be like if we were ever actually buried by the Reds. Safe thinking appeared to be a primary (albeit tacit) goal of the school system's curriculum. We practiced air-raid drills, with grim-faced mothers shuttling us from our schools to the site of future bomb shelters. I remember watching Nikita Khrushchev on national television pounding his shoe on the table. I hoped that the world would see that we Americans were rational and controlled, more "morally correct," and would thus support us in what then seemed an archetypally important race.

While I was learning to protect myself and my country from communism, however, the Black students in my hometown were strictly segregated in the vocational high school, most of them learning to be

5

beauticians or auto mechanics. They were trained primarily to serve and to entertain. They didn't have a communications course in their curriculum, but they did have an outstanding football team and marching band. I knew this not because my high school ever played theirs in football, but because I read about their games in the newspaper and saw them perform every year in the Christmas parade.

The public schools were not integrated until 1969. I had finished a master's degree in education by then and had come back home as one of the first White teachers in an all-Black elementary school. The year proved difficult for me and my students. It was sobering to discover that the school in which I found myself teaching and the schools I had attended were part of the same school system. The difference in quality between the education and resources available to my students and those that had been available to me and my friends was profound. My pleasant memories of growing up and the excitement of learning were placed in a different perspective after that first year of teaching. Since then I have not been able to remember those years without thinking about the "other" children in our town who were afforded such narrow opportunity.

Years later I look back on the late 1950s and early 1960s, both in my own life and in our nation's history, with a more critical eye. Fear of the communist threat and the strong racial and regional divisions I experienced as a child seem to have been driven by an obsession with the "Other" — an obsession that survives today by shaping notions of what literacy is, who should have it, and for what purposes.

From the Cold War to the War on Illiteracy

Although I have lived most of my life in the company of the cold war, recent events in Eastern Europe and what used to be known as the Soviet Union have dissolved the object of those posturings. These changes have allowed attention to shift to new issues, or old issues in new disguises. Instead of fighting the Other abroad, there is a rush to fight the Other at home. The transition from the cold war to the war on illiteracy gained momentum in the early 1980s, with the appearance of a wide range of dire predictions and sobering commission reports. Published in 1983 were *A Nation at Risk, Action for Excellence*, and *Educating America for the Twenty-first Century*, each of which portrayed the decline and fall of the American educational system. Coincidentally, 1983 also marked the publication of Heath's *Ways with Words* and Giroux's *Theory and Resistance in Education*, two books that suggest very different ways of interpreting current educational policy, practice, and outcomes.

By 1987, the literacy crisis had expanded to include alarm over the literacy skills of current and future workers. *Workforce 2000* (Johnston & Packer, 1987) was published that year, and it has influenced policy-makers and pundits ever since. The thesis of *Workforce 2000* predicts a coming shortage of skilled workers just when jobs will require a more highly skilled labor force. The report blames schools, students, and workers for this problem and suggests that leadership from the private sector can solve it with minimal financial help from government. The Other is no longer the Communists but an undereducated workforce, and the schools are responsible for this undereducation. The threat is no longer militaristic, it is economic. But apocalyptic visions still emerge from unacceptable levels of literacy, and war metaphors are still used to describe the problem as well as its proposed solutions.

The general argument is that schools are failing to provide business, industry, and the military with adults capable of performing adequately in their jobs. When declining birthrates and increasing immigration are considered, we are left with grim predictions: not enough literate workers to fill available jobs, not enough literate workers to support the baby-boom generation as it moves closer to retirement, not enough literate workers to allow business and industry to compete in an increasingly global market (Chisman, 1989). According to Philippi (1988), this situation will lead to the development of a two-tiered society by the year 2000: one group that wants to and is able to work and another group that lacks the basic skills to be employed at any level. Indeed, analysts such as Cornell (1988) predict that jobs requiring only basic literacy skills will soon disappear.

The media have found that the literacy crisis provides compelling copy. They energetically hawk the "raging debate" (Pendered, 1991), the "most pressing need" (Staff, 1989), the "illiteracy epidemic" (Zuckerman, 1989). There has emerged what Hull (1991) has described as a unique "public discourse" (p. 2) surrounding workplace literacy. This discourse is constructed to be (and is) powerfully alarming.

Also employing the public discourse of a literacy crisis are volunteer organizations, which actively seek both helpers and those willing to define themselves as in need of help. Federal, state, and private funding for literacy programs has grown slowly, but steadily. In short, there has developed a social "rescue" policy (Quigley, 1991, p. 33) to save both the unlettered and the nation from certain ruin. The perception of a literacy crisis has become a major organizing symbol in the workplace and the broader community, and response to the crisis has become a major economic (and scholarly) commodity. Like the deficit theories of the 1960s and 1970s, it has also served to deflect public attention from a complexity of social and economic issues the nation seems unwilling or unable to address.

A Closer Look

In order to analyze this talk about workplace literacy, it is helpful to consider the conditions on which the claim of "crisis" have been based. Three specific changes are generally cited as causing this critical juncture. One of the dominant themes in this discussion is that the shift to an information economy employing advanced technology requires highly skilled workers. Another theme involves the significant shifts in the ethnic and gender distribution as well as the size of the future workforce. And finally, there is the familiar contention that the nation is in the throes of a major decline in basic skills: The infidels are at the gates, and we are going to have to let them in to run the computers. A closer look at the research on these issues, however, suggests the possibility of a different interpretation.

The Unspoken Effects of Technology

There is no disputing that technology has generated some dramatic changes in what work is and how it is performed. Yet if one examines the data on work and workers, the most significant effect of this technology appears to be the elimination of many jobs and the de-skilling of the jobs that remain after the change. When several old jobs are absorbed into a single new one, the result is several displaced workers with very specialized (and often no longer marketable) knowledge. The skills required in the new job are broader but not as specialized.

The public discourse often describes these "high-skilled" jobs as requiring workers who can perform in organizations that emphasize participatory management, increased product quality, and customer satisfaction. Yet 95 percent of American workplaces are not currently structured to create such a setting (National Center on Education and the Economy, 1990, p. 3). Moreover, the wages for many "new" jobs are much lower, and many workers are left with no jobs at all. This elimination and de-skilling is seldom discussed in the popular discourse, although there is a growing body of published data to support these conclusions. (For reviews of these data, see National Center on Education and the Economy, 1990; Mishel & Teixeira, 1991. See also Kazemek, 1988; Rachleff, 1991; Stone, 1991.) In addition, as technological transformations accelerate, institutions will probably change more rapidly, requiring workers with even more flexible (and less specialized) skills and the ability to change jobs or even industries several times during their adult years. This, in turn, will require workers to take more responsibility for their own employability rather than relying on one company for a lifetime position (Carnevale, Gainer & Meltzer, 1990).

Thus, technological changes in the workplace have several consequences. There are fewer jobs available, and those that are available are often de-skilled. As a result, real earned income has steadily decreased over the last two decades. Between 1978 and 1990, for example, real earned income of American workers fell by 11 percent, and between 1982 and 1988, outstanding household debt escalated from 75 percent to 94 percent of after-tax income. Moreover, health care benefits have steadily decreased, and 37 million Americans lack any health care coverage whatsoever. At the same time, jobs are becoming increasingly dangerous. In this nation 300 workers die each day from job-related injury or disease (Rachleff, 1991). These changes appear to be continuing at an increasingly accelerated pace. Technology is not only transforming the skills required to perform jobs and the number of jobs available, but requiring the development of new life coping skills as well.

Yet some analysts claim that American business, with its eyes on short-term profits, has done little to prepare itself or its employees for these changes. In general, ways of thinking about skills and knowledge as well as the modes of production developed at the turn of the century are still the preferred model in the American workplace. Tasks are broken up into small, discrete units, and employees are trained to perform these tasks with great precision. Organizational structures mirror this assembly-line approach. Companies often rely on layers of highly skilled, well-paid administrators to manage large numbers of employees with only the basic skills necessary for front-line work. This model of management, developed by Frederick W. Taylor (Whyte, 1992) at the turn of the century, is still the preferred model not only in manufacturing but also in service industries such as banking and health care.

Technology may actually have changed some methods of production, but surprisingly, the data suggest that the general consensus of most management is that while other businesses have trouble with underskilled employees, their own employees possess the skills needed to perform with competence. In a survey conducted by the National Center on Education and the Economy (1990), 95 percent of the employers responded that most of their employees already possessed adequate skills to perform their current jobs, and they foresaw little change in the level of skills needed to perform jobs in the future. When asked about a literacy crisis, they agreed that it was a problem in other sectors of the economy, but not with their own workers. The skills they did cite as in need of improvement included social skills such as being pleasant, hardworking, and reliable.

Furthermore, and perhaps because they perceive no need, management does comparatively little in terms of supporting worker education with real dollars. The Office of Technology Assessment's *Worker Training: Competing in the New International Economy* (1990) claims that corporate America spends between $30 and $44 billion on worker training each year. Yet this amount is not distributed evenly across all companies: $27 billion is spent by 0.5 percent of U.S. employers, and only 100 to 200 employers spend more than 2 percent of their payrolls on employee training programs. The vast majority spend little or nothing on formal training for their employees.

When we examine how those companies that do spend money on training distribute those dollars, the picture becomes even more interesting. Two-thirds of the total funds spent on training are spent on college-educated employees, while front-line workers receive comparatively little training. Training focused specifically on upgrading basic literacy skills is relatively uncommon. Spending on literacy programs by U.S. companies, the government, and unions adds up to only about $1 billion per year, which is only about 3 percent of the total funds spent on training annually (Stone, 1991).

Thus, we have a major contradiction between the public discourse on literacy in the workplace and the actual spending and management patterns of U.S. employers. Although there is much talk about upgrading basic skills, there is comparatively little action. And those workers who are commonly defined as most in need of training are least likely to receive it.

Demographic Shifts

The second major change often cited as contributing to a literacy crisis is the demographic shift occurring in the labor pool. The number of 16- to 24-year-olds entering the job market is shrinking each year and will continue to do so for several more years. This is forcing employers to hire from "groups where historically human resource development has been deficient" (Carnevale et al., no date, p. ii) — a euphemism for the growing numbers of Blacks, Hispanics, and women in the workforce.

In fact, it is estimated that by the year 2000, 80 percent of the new workforce will be women, minorities, and immigrants. This especially concerns employers, who believe that there will be too few well-educated and trained workers to fill available jobs. In the past, employers have had a large labor pool of qualified candidates (mostly White males) from which to choose, but changing demographics have narrowed those choices considerably. Employers (also primarily White males) often voice concern that this diverse labor pool (the Other) will not be skilled enough to perform the jobs available. Consider, for example, this observation in *Business Week* (September 1989):

> White, non-Hispanic men, once regarded as the prime working group, will make up less than 10 percent of the entering labor force. Thus, in a time of labor shortages, when U.S. companies will require increasingly educated workers to compete in world markets, more and more workers are likely to lack basic skills. (p. 242)

It is important to examine carefully the implications of these shifting demographics. Minority groups and women historically have received far fewer educational opportunities than have White males. Thus the overall level of basic skills of the current workforce may have declined because it is composed of fewer White middle-class males, who generally have had better access to adequate educational opportunities than do women and minorities. It is thus possible for the level of skills of the overall workforce to decline while the basic skills of groups constituting increasingly larger segments of the current workforce have stayed the same or even risen.

To understand the implications of this changing labor pool, let's examine some of the current research on educational attainment. First, according to a recent report from the National Assessment of Educational Progress (NAEP)(Mullis, Owen & Phillips, 1990), achievement levels of Black and Hispanic youth have improved significantly in the last two decades, although the gap between these groups and White youth is still troublingly large.

The story of women's educational achievement is even more interesting. According to the NAEP report, differences in performance between male and female students have remained the same over the last 20 years. However, this report examines scholastic attainment only in grades four, eight, and twelve. A report by the U.S. Department of Education, *Women at Thirtysomething: Paradoxes of Attainment* (Adelman, 1991), suggests that women have made steady and significant gains in their educational abilities and their work-related skills, but have received comparatively little in the way of economic reward for this attainment. In this study of the high school graduating class of 1972, women had achieved pay equity with men in only 7 of 33 major occupations. And between the ages of 25 and 32 these women experienced a much higher percentage of unemployment than did men regardless of credentials earned.

Perceived Deficiency/Decline in Basic Skills

The current literacy crisis is rooted in the perception of a vast erosion in the educational system, which has resulted in workers who are ill prepared to perform. Most of these discussions of current literacy are couched in the language of decline or deficit. In one set of scenarios, worker skills have declined steadily since the "good old days." A call for a return to the "basics" accompanies this position. Students can no longer read, write, and compute. In addition, schools are no longer training students to be productive and efficient workers. Education must return to traditional values and practices in order to increase basic skills levels. "Education," observes DeMarco (1990), "as practiced by the schools, is not just a failure but a hopeless undertaking" (p. 16).

A somewhat related set of scenarios suggests that workers have always been deficient, but more sophisticated technology is only now pinpointing the problem. For example, *The Bottom Line*, a federal publication on workplace literacy problems and solutions, suggests that "New technology has changed the nature of work—created new jobs and altered others—and, in many cases, *has revealed basic skills problems among experienced, older employees where none were known to exist*" (1988, p. 3; emphasis added). Thus employees have had skills deficiencies all along, but it has taken a more sophisticated workplace to uncover them. In this position there is no decline, but rather an inherent deficiency only now being discovered.

Data from the NAEP suggest that this viewpoint is simply wrong. According to the study, student achievement over the last 20 years has remained constant. In the basic literacy skills of reading, writing, and mathematics, there has been virtually no significant change. In science and social studies, students declined in the 1970s but improved in the 1980s. What has changed is not educational attainment, but the demands of the workplace.

Yet, in putting the onus on the individual and the schools for producing deficient workers, the public discourse carefully avoids the notion that perhaps the workplace itself and how workers are positioned in the workplace need to be restructured. Thus, as the workplace becomes more complex and competitive, and perhaps less humane, workers are called on to adjust to rapid change and to use the skills that they should have had all along—skills the workplace never required before and that employers seem reluctant to help them acquire.

Blaming schools and individuals for the economic problems of the nation diverts attention from the outdated modes of production and management as well as the lack of financial and structural support for worker training that still characterize much of the American workplace. Erickson (1988) suggests that it also hides the fact that for much of the century, schools have been doing exactly what the culture has intended them to do: sort students into categories based on class and ethnicity and arm them with a discrete set of quantifiably measured literacy skills to perform in a hierarchically controlled mass-market economy. (For further examination of the sorting system in American education, see Wilcox, 1982.)

A Broader Perspective

In order to explore the current public discourse of a workplace literacy crisis, we must not only examine current statistical research but also consider the broader social and historical contexts out of which it arises. First, the nation is experiencing deep-seated change on many levels. When major social change occurs, the *perception* of a literacy crisis is often one of the first indicators. Indeed, Graff (1987) maintains that this is a pattern throughout development in the West: "At times of large-scale, rapid change and confusion about the condition of civilization and morality, literacy has seemed to suffer a 'decline' almost generally across the span of recorded history" (p. 373).

Literacy, Education, and Work

When we examine the development of literacy and education in the West, we discover that attending school to become a successful worker is a relatively new use of education and of literacy skills. Before the industrial revolution, many occupations required little or no formalized reading, writing, or mathematics. Work was often performed at home or on the land, and the skills necessary to learn an occupation were acquired by the apprenticeship model of watching, listening, and practicing with a parent or master craftsperson. Education and literacy were frequently acquired at home or at church for the salvation of one's soul rather than for the economic advancement of one's country.

Specific examples of mass literacy campaigns can be seen as early as the 1500s. In these early campaigns, literacy was fostered to develop religious piety and national unity rather than to produce skilled workers (Gawthrop, 1987; Houston, 1987; Johansson, 1981). Literacy was tied directly to religion and morality in colonial New England as well. Lockridge (1974) maintains, however, that there is little evidence to support claims that high levels of literacy led to individual economic or social advancement. Graff (1979) reached the same conclusions in his study of nineteenth-century Ontario towns. In the eighteenth and early nineteenth centuries in America, literacy was promoted as the means to ensure that all citizens read a narrowly prescribed set of religious texts and fulfilled their responsibilities as citizens of the republic, not as a means of acquiring or displaying new information (Resnick & Resnick, 1977). Thus literacy was not a skill required in the workplace but rather a broader set of behaviors that individuals used to act in culturally appropriate ways.

The Factory Model of Schooling

With the rise of industrialization and the strong influence of science, however, mass schooling came to be seen as a way to develop the kind of obedient, compliant workers needed to labor in the mills and factories. "[T]he process of becoming literate was itself a process of socialization promulgated by those interested in using the schools to resolve the social, economic, and political tensions arising from a culturally pluralistic and emerging industrial society" (Stevens, 1987, p. 99). (It is difficult to untangle the rather complicated relationship between literacy and schooling. For a detailed discussion of this problem, see Scribner & Cole, 1981.) The goals of mass schooling appear to have been to stem the tide of "crime, poverty, and immorality" (de Castell & Luke, 1988, p. 162).

Thus, in response to rapid social and economic change, schools at the beginning of the twentieth century provided "the skills, knowledge, and social attitudes for urbanized commercial and industrial society" (de Castell & Luke, 1988, p. 166). Educational texts such as the Bible and the classics were replaced with those extolling the virtues of technology and commercialism. Following Dewey's "progressivism," children read texts that were socially descriptive rather than morally prescriptive. Industrial methods of instruction replaced more classical methods of rote memorization and oral recitation. Organization replaced conversation, and literacy skills replaced literate behaviors (Heath, 1990). Schools became physical plants and were managed according to sound business principles. Thus, literacy and schooling became closely linked with work and with competence in the workplace.

As schools implemented a scientific, behavioristic approach focused on testing students' ability to acquire and display discrete bits of isolated information, they reproduced the characteristics of the workplace. Thus, the ways literacy skills have been defined, tested, and measured reflect and have been reflected, for most of the century, by the nation's modes of production and beliefs about what constitutes knowledge. If there is a crisis in the workplace, it is not simply the result of a poor educational system, increased technology, changing demographics, and declining basic skills. Rather, the means of production and the definitions of what constitutes knowledge, which schools reflect in their curriculum and pedagogy, are no longer providing effective strategies for survival in a rapidly changing world.

Possible Solutions

A solution is generally offered to a problem based on how the problem is defined. As we have seen, the public discourse about workplace literacy defines the problem in a particular way, but some analysts and critics adopt other definitions of the problem and thus allow for other solutions. For example, approaches to improving workforce literacy generally range from skills-oriented training programs using phonics (Pendered, 1991), to functional context approaches (Sticht, Armstrong, Hickey & Caylor 1987; Philippi, 1991), to worker-centered approaches (Sarmiento & Kay, 1990; Soifer, Irwin, Crumrine, Honzaki, Simmons & Young, 1990), to suggestions for a major restructuring of the entire workplace (National Center on Education and the Economy, 1990; Stone, 1991).

The Functional Context/Literacy Audit Approach

In 1988, when the King Memorial project was developed, the most popular of these approaches was the functional context approach using a "literacy audit" or "general task analysis" to determine the literacy skills required for specific job tasks and to develop curriculum based on these skills. The funding agency suggested that this approach be used to develop curriculum for the King Memorial project. Several publications describe various formulations of this approach, including *The Bottom Line: Basic Skills in the Workplace* (1988), *Workplace Basics: The Essential Skills Employers Want* (Carnevale, Gainer & Meltzer, 1990), *Upgrading Basic Skills for the Workplace* (1989), and *Literacy at Work: The Workbook for Program Developers* (Philippi, 1991). These strategies have been marketed to the business community as a way to improve quality control and productivity by improving worker performance. At least one vendor claims that it can cut the time needed for training by as much as 50 percent and that work performance will be improved on a variety of *quantitative* measures (e.g., Simon & Schuster's promotional literature on Philippi, 1991). Hull, in a review of these materials (1991), suggests that "a whole new mini-industry of manuals and workbook instruction" has evolved around functional context approaches (p. 8).

The literacy audit, the centerpiece of much functional context curriculum, is a process whereby observation, interviews, and the collection of written materials are used to determine the literacy skills supposedly "embedded" in specific job tasks. This audit assumes that employees and supervisors explicitly know and can explain in step-by-step sequence what skills are needed to perform a job well. It further assumes that the auditor will be able to recognize and describe literate behaviors in the same ways employees and supervisors do and then construct ways to measure these behaviors. These two assumptions conflict with current research (Cook-Gumperz, 1986; Heath, 1983; Lave, 1988; Scribner & Sachs, 1990; Sachs, 1991), which suggests that knowledge about process is often more tacit than explicit, that it does not necessarily transfer from one task to another or one context to another, that it is socially and culturally constructed, and that it is not always conceived of in linear, sequential detail.

It is informative, in considering this approach to literacy instruction, to consider where the process originated and how it has come to be so popular. The term *functional* associated with literacy was first used in the 1930s by the Civilian Conservation Corps. It was defined as the attainment of at least three years of schooling (Rose, 1989). By the end of World War II, and as a result of the use of standardized testing in the military, functional literacy generally referred to the ability "to understand instructions necessary for conducting necessary military functions and tasks" (de Castell & Luke, 1988, p. 169). The results of massive standardized testing during World War II led policymakers to conclude that despite universal schooling, many adult males were not functionally literate. As a result, the military, along with educational consultants, began to develop functional context strategies to upgrade the basic skills of its recruits. These strategies were quite successful and in the 1980s began to be applied to business and industrial settings as well (Philippi, 1988; Sticht et al., 1987).

Functional context not only assumes certain characteristics about knowledge, it also supports specific assessment measures. What constitutes a literacy skill and how that skill is measured are both directly tied to quantifiable measures of specific job tasks. It is a model well-suited to industrial modes of production because it is driven by the same set of industrial and behavioristic assumptions about knowledge that separate skills into discrete categories and emphasize the linearity and hierarchy of tasks involved in production. Improved productivity comes from enhanced precision in the execution of job tasks.

The Worker-Centered Approach

As background for this study it is also important to understand other approaches that are used to teach adults in the workplace and the theoretical frameworks that inform them. The method most often used instead of functional context is worker- or learner-centered instruction and is generally informed by theories of whole language and participatory education (Freire & Macedo, 1987; Goodman, Goodman & Hood, 1989; Moffet, 1985; Sarmiento & Kay, 1990; Soifer et al., 1990). In many instances, of course, practitioners borrow from a variety of approaches to fashion programs based on "what works" (see, for example, North, 1987, for a discussion of the pragmatic strategies practitioners often employ in language education).

Whole language theory rests on the assumption that individuals learn best when they have control of the learning process and when they define the skills to be learned. It is related to the somewhat controversial position from the 1970s that each learner has a right to his or her own language. The political dimensions of this approach are self-evident. Whole language approaches are grounded in the cultural identity of the individual and work to develop literacy from within that location rather than by imposing a set of external, objective strategies for acquiring and displaying knowledge. Moreover, whole language proponents argue that students learn best when they move from the authentic expressions of their own language — the whole — to the part and that these authentic expressions *vary* across individuals as well as across settings. This is in direct contrast to industrial models of learning, which rest on the assumption described above that learning takes place when a student moves from the part — the discrete, isolated skills of literacy — to the whole. Assessment measures in whole language programs are often qualitative and thus based on learner performance as evidenced by portfolios, journals, collaborative group learning projects, interviews, and self-evaluation. One of the best applications of whole language theory to adult literacy instruction can be found in Soifer et al. (1990).

We can understand the underlying conflict between functional context and whole language by thinking of them as modes of production. The functional context approach, especially its emphasis on literacy audits and job tasks, fits nicely with industrial models and assembly-line techniques. Whole language fits with a mode of production that emphasizes redistributions of power in the decision-making process through flattened hierarchies, work teams, and participatory management. Stein and Sperazi (1991) have developed a description of the kinds of literacy approaches that would be best suited for various kinds of work settings. For example, a functional context approach with a detailed literacy audit that focuses on job tasks might fit with the goals of more traditional workplaces bent on increasing productivity by improving current practice. In contrast, an approach like whole language, which emphasizes learner-centered instruction, may be better suited to workplaces interested in transforming their modes of production as well as their methods of management. In reality, most work environments are a complex mix of these two extremes. For example, in the King Memorial project, theoretical and political frameworks were varied and often conflicted. It is the tensions between these competing theories of making, displaying, and measuring knowledge and the application of these theories in a specific workplace literacy program that the remainder of this book addresses. Come back with me now to the beginning of this project and join me as I begin to hear and see the unfolding of a unique story about the women and men who play the various roles in the drama of a national crisis.

The King Memorial Project

When the King Memorial begins, I am a novice. I want to analyze what happens when adults become literate, and I wonder how the literacy program might (or might not) change the women and men who will participate in it. But I do not realize that my own life will change significantly as well. I am aware of the fallacy of the "Great Divide" theories (Walters, 1990, p. 174), but I do not have a clear understanding of the concrete ways in which dualism can be played out in a workplace setting. In addition, although I teach composition and reading to underprepared college students, I have little training in adult or vocational education.

I soon realize, however, that this lack of knowledge gives me a certain advantage. I am able to enter the field without preconceived notions about workplace literacy programs or the teaching of adults. On this level, it is not difficult to "make the familiar strange." Much of what

I will observe in the following 11 months is new and unfamiliar. On another level, however, the familiar becomes very strange indeed.

Site of Data Collection

The King Memorial Work Skills Development Program (WSDP) is coordinated by Bayside University's Adult Literacy Resources Center (ALRC). The center is housed off campus in a large office building not too far from the hospital. Although the instruction is conducted at the hospital, the meetings with staff and consultants, as well as the lesson planning and all the data analysis are conducted at the center. The hospital, which is described in detail in Chapter 3, and the ALRC serve as the primary sites for data collection. I spend a great deal of time at the center both before and after the literacy project is implemented. During the nine months that the literacy classes are in session, I spend more time at the hospital and eventually at other locations with program participants.

Participants in the Study

The men and women who participate in the study are the hospital employees working in housekeeping, food service, and laundry. They are all African-American and range in age from 19 to 63. I also observe and interview other individuals at the hospital including the supervisors, managers, and personnel staff.

The staff members of ALRC, from the director to the volunteer tutors, also play important roles in this study. Table 1.1 describes personnel associated with the project. The director of the King Memorial

Table 1.1: ALRC Staff and Other Personnel

Name	Title	Duties
Noreen	Director of ALRC	Development Assessment
Karen	Assistant Director	Development Curriculum
Aisha	Instructor	Curriculum Recruitment Teaching
Rose	Research Assistant	Assessment Tutoring
Amanda and Sarah	Volunteer Tutors	Tutoring
Margaret, Roberta, and Ann-Marie	Consultants	Development Evaluation

project is Noreen Johnston and the assistant director is Karen Anderson — both White middle-class academics with terminal degrees in education. Each has a special interest in reading instruction, although neither has been trained in adult education. Noreen is in charge of the evaluation component of the King project, and Karen is in charge of the curriculum development. Noreen and Karen spend most of their time at the center or the university.

Noreen and Karen are important players in the drama I watch unfold, but the person who shares the most with me, who teaches me the most, and who reveals the most of herself is Aisha Samara, the instructional coordinator of the project. Noreen and Karen have hired Aisha to recruit the employees, teach the classes, and develop the curriculum. They have specifically chosen Aisha because she is African-American and well educated. They know that all the employees who will participate in the project will be African-American, and they want an instructor who will be able to work well within the culture. But Aisha, like Karen and Noreen, is from the middle class. Although she identifies herself as a member of the "Black community," as she calls it, she is not from the working class within that community. As a result, this study is a complex mix of race, gender, and class within a region that still upholds these divisions as elements of a stable community (see Fox-Genovese, 1991, for an analysis of this tendency in the South).

One might choose to call Aisha my "key informant," but that term does not accurately reflect the role she plays in my research or our relationship. She is more like a "border agent" who helps me negotiate my way into unfamiliar territory. Although she considers herself an academic and an intellectual, she seems to be more of an activist than any of the academics I know. She works as a consultant and a community organizer rather than as an employee of an institution. Her independence, overtly political stance, and her ability to improvise are all quite a change from the academic behaviors I have been socialized into. I find her an especially engaging woman.

But Aisha withholds her judgment about me for some time. Initially I do not realize the extent to which she mistrusts researchers, especially White women. Nor do I fully appreciate the deep-seated reasons for that mistrust. As I write this story, I now realize how delicate it is to establish trust when conducting research in the workplace. Those persons cast as the "subjects" have much to lose by participation in such a project.

Aisha has an office in the center during the months she works on the project. A reflection of her own personal and ethnic identity, it is an ever-shifting, colorful array of African art and artifacts, memorabilia of African-American women's special contributions to American culture, and stacks of papers, lesson plans, memoranda, phone messages, books, magazines, and perhaps a recipe or an extra pair of shoes. Her clothes are richly colored and her hair is often intricately braided and arranged. She teaches me a great deal about the African-American community and the unique qualities of African-American women.

Another important player in this drama is Rose Mitchell, who joins the center as a graduate research assistant shortly after the project begins. A former high school Latin teacher, Rose is just beginning work on a doctoral degree in education. Rose's ways of organizing time and space are very methodical. Neat, orderly, and organized, her desk and work area are always clutter free, each item filed or stored in its proper place. Above her desk are pictures of the roses she grows in her garden and often brings in for the ALRC staff to enjoy. She is an excellent record keeper, and as she becomes more and more invested in the project, she takes on many of the daily details that its implementation requires. She is responsible for a large portion of the assessment measures and data analysis.

Two women who volunteer to help tutor in the project also become key players in the study. Amanda appears serendipitously at the center on the day Aisha sets aside to train volunteers. She eventually goes on to teach a class for supervisors that the hospital management requests. A highly trained academic, she dropped out of her graduate program just short of obtaining her doctoral degree. She talks of how she has made a conscious decision "to say yes to life, and institutions don't say yes to life." Amanda generally operates outside the constraints of the academy that defines the professional lives of Noreen, Karen, Rose, and myself. This fresh perspective is quite helpful in the data collection and analysis process. Amanda has no stake in the study other than her modest salary. She has no long-term commitments to the center or the university, and her views are often quite different from those of others involved in the project.

Sarah also stands outside the project as a doctoral student at another institution, so her relationship to the center and its sponsoring university is not constrained by her position as a student. She comes to the center as a volunteer with a great deal of expertise in curriculum development and teaching experience. Her outsider's role is also quite helpful in the data collection and analysis.

Outside Consultants

During the course of the project, the entire project staff meets with various outside consultants to discuss problems, possible solutions, and strategies. These consultants include Ann-Marie (whole language),

Roberta (mathematics), and Margaret (functional context). Ann-Marie and Roberta contribute to the developmental stages of the project but have minimal involvement in curriculum development.

Margaret holds the most influence in developing lessons and materials. She represents one perspective on workplace literacy. Her definition of the problem and its solution fit within the public discourse about workplace literacy described earlier. Her goal is to help workers develop the skills necessary to survive in the current system and to advance within it. On the other hand, Aisha holds a very different conception of the problem and the solution. As a social activist with a background in self-help models and Freirean study groups, Aisha believes that the system needs to be changed. She sees the goal of workplace literacy instruction as empowerment through the development of a critical consciousness in order to change the current social, political, and economic system. In the middle, and being pulled in both directions for a variety of reasons, are Noreen, Karen, Rose, Amanda, and Sarah. As we shall see in the following chapters, these differences in the way the literacy problem is conceptualized by the various members of the project have a significant influence on the development and outcomes of the classes.

The Researcher's Role

Karen and Noreen see the need for an ethnographic component to their project, even though the grant provides no monies for such an analysis. In addition, they know that, given the institutional constraints of the dissertation process, I will be unable to share my results with them until the study is complete. The advisor for my dissertation is quite supportive of ethnographic research, but not of my full participation in an action-oriented project. I am instructed, therefore, to defer sharing my results until the completion of the study.

Knowing this requirement, Noreen still believes that my research will enhance the project, and her interest in and strong support of doctoral students makes it easy for me to negotiate initial entry into the project. But it is only a superficial ease. I ultimately have to negotiate and renegotiate through several levels as the project unfolds. This happens almost immediately with Aisha and with Karen as well. I eventually learn the significance of the following events, but at the time they occur, I am both puzzled and frustrated by them. Although Noreen tells me that I can have access to the literacy classes for the collection of much of my data, Aisha and Karen are reluctant to let me observe the classes. They are both afraid that too many "outsiders" taking notes will scare potential participants away from the classes. And when classes start with very low levels of employee participation, their fears escalate. Karen questions the wisdom of having a researcher in the classes. She is particularly interested in the project's success — in many ways she has more at stake than anyone else — and begins to think that outside researchers are a mistake. Karen, as a trained academic, envisions the same sort of researcher role that I do initially, the participant observer as observer. She does not see my role, nor do I, as an active agent in the classroom. Indeed, most of our academic training has taught us to spurn active participation as risking contamination or bias.

Aisha, however, expresses somewhat different reasons for concern. She wants me to take an active role in the classes, or no role at all. She strongly objects to having someone sit in the back of the room taking notes. She believes that uninvolved observation is "disrespectful, exploitive . . . not a way to be in the world." She explains to me that, "We owe them [the employees] more than that."

At the time, I think she is unsophisticated, but I later come to realize that Aisha has very little patience with academics who observe passively. To her mind, knowledge is something one *does*, not something one acquires and stockpiles. In later chapters, we shall see the implications for this view of making meaning. But in the beginning of the project, she simply tells me that she wants me to be a tutor — to actively engage in teaching and learning.

This is not the role I have envisioned, but I soon discover that taking an active role in the classroom enables me to develop close personal relationships with a few of the learners in the class. This, in turn, leads to invitations to church, home, and social events, which enables me to spend time with them in a variety of situations outside of work. The participants are cautious and protective at first, but by the end of the study they are eager to talk with me and often initiate conversations so that I can understand something more clearly.

During class, I sit with the learners and assist them with lessons as Aisha instructs me to do. I try not to initiate teaching activities on my own and constantly wait for direction from Aisha or later, from Rose, as to what I should do. In other words, I am as passive as I can be within my "active" role. I make every effort not to interfere in the lesson plans of the day and to behave as an assistant rather than as the person in charge of the class. This is a very difficult role for me. I come to the study with 20 years of teaching experience, and not to be in charge is a new challenge. In this role, however, I gain insight and understanding in ways that would never occur if I were more directive in class.

During the entire project, I struggle to be open to the behaviors and constructs of the other individuals. Ultimately, I begin to see contradictions between theory and action at work in the project. At times, this is very painful, especially when the individuals I am working with become angry or frustrated with one another. From my perspective, much of the conflict about methods and curriculum is a manifestation of radically different belief systems, but these differences are often interpreted as deficiency or even incompetence. To observe this and not try to fix it is difficult.

Another difficulty occurs in my role as tutor. In attempting to be a willing and active listener, I encourage the hospital employees to talk. This sometimes proves to be problematic. Unlike the tutors in the project, Aisha does not always follow the traditional formal school discourse of initiation, response, evaluation (IRE). Instead, she and the employees both tend to employ overlapping and co-speaking. Within this context, I am able to speak and listen to learners with ease, collecting very rich data. Other tutors, however, who are more comfortable with the IRE model of classroom discourse, are often annoyed when the employees and I talk in class about things that, in their opinion, are not on task. I find myself in the difficult position of wanting to be a good listener for the employees, which demands one kind of behavior, and a good tutor, which sometimes requires a different kind of behavior.

I often meet with Aisha to discuss the project over lunch or as we walk to and from the hospital. We talk on the phone often, and over time, Aisha invites me to several social functions with her friends. I attend farewell parties and celebration luncheons, learning valuable lessons about how she and her friends socialize, organize, and act within their communities. As we become good friends, my role as the involved, active tutor and my role as the researcher conducting a more traditional, uninvolved ethnography conflict. I find it difficult to resolve this conflict of roles over the course of the study.

Methods of Data Collection

The methods of data collection vary across the 11 months of the study. (See Table 1.2 for a time line and description of data collection.) I begin collecting data on the literacy project in October as Noreen and Karen are preparing to initiate the project and hire the needed personnel. I observe as they meet with hospital management to discuss the needs of the employees and the goals of the program. After the classes begin, I serve as a tutor to the classes that meet each Monday and Thursday from 5:00 to 6:30 PM for nine months. I also meet with some of the employees on Wednesday evenings for extra tutoring sessions. I

Table 1.2.   Time Line and Data-Collection Procedures

Time	Site	Types of Data Collected
10/88–1/89	ALRC	Field notes, Artifacts
	Hospital	Field notes, Artifacts
2/89–5/89	ALRC	Field notes, Artifacts
	Hospital	Field notes, Artifacts
	Classes	Field notes, Artifacts
5/89–9/89	ALRC	Field notes, Artifacts, Tapes
	Hospital	Field notes, Artifacts
	Classes	Field notes, Artifacts, Tapes
	Homes	Field notes, Tapes
	Churches	Field notes, Artifacts, Tapes
	Community	Field notes, Artifacts, Tapes

take notes on these meetings for several months before I start using a tape recorder in interviews, class sessions, and staff meetings. (Tape recording from the beginning of the project would be ideal, but it also would make the program participants quite uneasy. Unlike the school setting I am more familiar with, the hospital is a place where privacy is protected, and people with tape recorders are viewed with a great deal of suspicion. I never consider videotaping class segments. This would be much too intrusive a measure in a situation in which very little trust exists. I do eventually arrange for some videotaping of interviews after the program is completed. These are conducted at Aisha's home and are not part of ALRC's project.)

I also spend time on my own in the hospital cafeterias, elevators, and corridors eating, listening, reading bulletin boards, and just hanging out in order to understand the hospital culture. During preliminary fieldwork the extent of my hospital observations is arbitrary, depending on the comfort level of various project personnel. When I move into the formal stage of the study, I spend two to three days each week observing in these three areas of the hospital, as project scheduling and the willingness of participants allow. In addition, as the study is nearing completion, I begin working in one of the critical care units in the hospital to gain firsthand knowledge of King Memorial from my own perspective.

The categories that emerge from the preliminary data collection set the course of the study and help refine the questions that then guide the remainder of the data collection and analysis. The unit of analysis in the preliminary stages of the study is the individual learner. But as the data collection progresses, it becomes apparent that the unit of analysis will

Table 1.3.   Themes Analyzed Across Units

Themes	Units
Defining literate behaviors	1,2,3,4
Defining competence	1,2,3,4
Worker/employer relations	2,3,4
Interpreting resistance	2,3,4
Making and displaying knowledge	1,2,3,4
Setting goals	1,2,3,4
Assessing outcomes	1,3,4

Key: 1 Funding agency, consultants, and ALRC staff
       (Noreen, Karen, Rose)
     2 Hospital management
     3 Instructors and tutors (Aisha, Amanda, Sarah)
     4 Employees

be tied to groups with differing stakes in the program. Thus, the funding agency, the academic/research staff at ALRC, and the outside consultants become one unit of analysis. The management at the hospital becomes another unit of analysis. The instructional staff at ALRC (Aisha, Amanda, Sarah) becomes the fourth unit of analysis, and the employees themselves become the final unit of analysis. Within each of these units, themes emerge that are compared across units (see Table 1.3).

Guiding Questions

From these themes emerge a series of questions that the public discourse on workplace literacy has generally failed to address:

1. How do these workers see their roles in the workplace? What social, economic, and historical forces shape these beliefs?
2. What skills do these workers believe they need to perform their work? What skills do these workers believe they need to advance at work?
3. How do these workers view their previous educational experiences?
4. In what ways do these workers define success?
5. In what ways do these workers use text at work and in other areas of their lives?
6. What do these workers want in a workplace literacy program? To what extent does the King Memorial program meet their needs?

7. How do these workers acquire and display knowledge?
8. How do the other players (with different levels of power) view these same issues? How do the tensions between the various groups' answers to these questions affect the literacy program?

In brief, how are beliefs about language, learning, and work shaped by the variety of interests in the program?

The next chapter introduces the voices I first hear in the study. As we shall see, these voices speak of high expectations and unforeseen difficulties. They serve to underscore the fact that there is no simple agreement on what literacy is, how one achieves it, and whose interests are served in its use.

CHAPTER 2

Hearing Voices

This study is not only one of stories, but of different stories about the same people, places, and circumstances. As a researcher, my aim is to hear the stories of the workers involved in the literacy program. But I begin collecting data about the study long before I meet any of these individuals. I begin by listening to the academics and consultants responsible for the development of the program. During this time, I also hear the stories of the hospital managers and supervisors, and as I listen to these groups, I hear familiar themes and common assumptions. But these are not harmonious stories. Subtle tensions and veiled conflicts leave the stories unfinished, confusing. And when I finally hear the workers' stories, I am invited into a world of inversion where familiar definitions of knowledge and competence are gradually turned upside down.

Thus the overarching themes of this study emerge from conflict and contradiction, with a cacophony of voices inviting multiple interpretations of singular events. Hearing this rich variety is both intriguing and confusing.

MANAGEMENT'S STORY:
"These people just don't know what they're doing"

In October and November, during the start-up phase of the study, center staff meets with hospital management to determine management's perception of the workers' literacy needs and what skills management believes will lead to improved job performance. Significantly, there is no employee representation in this initial stage.

In the first meeting with Ms. Bronson, the assistant director of the hospital, and her two assistants, Mr. Thomas and Mr. Johnson, several

Table 2.1. Management's Beliefs About Workers

Skill Deficiency	Resultant Behaviors
Unable to read	Confused
	Arbitrary
	Difficult to monitor
	Unable to follow directions
	Threatened by print
Relies on speaking and listening	Less attentive
	Less productive
	Less predictable
	Requires more supervision
Unable to write	Unable to display information in a formalized manner

concerns emerge. Table 2.1 summarizes those concerns. The managers explain that most of the "low-level" employees are "threatened by too much reading." For example, there are manuals that describe jobs, but the employees "seem to rely on learning orally from supervisors and other, more experienced workers." The printed materials that are available are used primarily by supervisors. "We post a 'Weekly Tips' sheet [in housekeeping] but staff seldom comprehend it," Ms. Bronson explains.

In the next meeting, with yet another round of managers, this concern is also echoed by Mr. Parrott, the director of the housekeeping staff and author of "Weekly Tips." He expresses frustration that employees do not read his weekly handout on the proper ways to clean. He is equally concerned that the other texts in the hospital are also ignored, especially the notebooks full of information stacked in his office. The kitchen manager, Mr. Lewis, complains that the workers seldom follow the recipes, but improvise instead, making substitutions too freely. He also suggests that literacy skills will aid them with "parenting skills" such as helping children with homework or negotiating with schools and health care providers. In general, management is concerned about workers who seem unable to read the texts it perceives as necessary for them to function effectively in their jobs. Ms. Bronson sums it all up by declaring that, "These people just don't know what they're doing."

She is especially concerned that written information needs to be reinforced orally. She perceives this need for oral communication of official policy as a serious problem. Information is conveyed in print by various means, including memos, training manuals, newsletters, and flyers. She expects employees to understand and act upon this information, but, as she explains, "Then we're still not sure they got it. Written notices are just not enough." There are similar complaints from supervisors. Management believes that employees will also perform more efficiently if they can read well enough to comprehend information in written form. Ms. Bronson explains that if employees understand their benefits package, for example, they will not spend so much time on the job asking one another questions and discussing changes in policy. She believes that if employees could read, they would be more quiet, less likely to talk during their work, and hence more productive.

In addition, management is concerned that front-line supervisors do not know how to fill out the forms used to "write someone up" — the grievance reports that are kept in employee files. As Ms. Bronson explains, "They can't even fill out forms correctly. It is both hard and intimidating." Most of the writing that entry-level and front-line supervisory personnel are called on to do is of a highly structured nature, including filling out forms, charts, and checklists. This kind of knowledge display is formalized, decontextualized, linear, and hierarchical. Many supervisors also complain that employees have a particularly difficult time when they write narratives, such as to report a breach of security or a job-related accident.

In this initial meeting, management suggests that employees who improve their basic skills will have the opportunity to be promoted to higher positions in the hospital. Mr. Johnson explains that he sees the need for employees to have "training to move up the ladder in their own field or in another field like area clerk. Some lower-level employees could do this if they had some basic skills." No mention is made of any other criteria used for promotion. The emphasis is on job performance and the literacy skills required to perform the jobs adequately. If the employees do not possess these skills, they can probably function "day to day, but they can't go anywhere." Ms. Bronson expresses pride in the fact that the hospital is a place where there is opportunity for advancement and where the personnel department prefers to promote from within if employees have the skills to function in higher-level positions. "Promotion from within is really good at King Memorial," she assures us.

To summarize, management at King Memorial wants entry-level employees to follow directions with consistency and a minimum of discussion or oral feedback. They believe that literacy training will make workers more quiet; less reliant on oral, face-to-face communication; and more reliant on text, especially the text created and disseminated by management. Being more reliant on text will, in turn, make employees more productive and efficient. In addition, employees with higher status need to be able to write up grievances and reprimands to discipline employees who break the rules.

Underlying these requirements is a closely held belief in the power of literacy to control employee behavior. Management at King Memorial presumes that literate workers will be more productive, more responsive to direction, and more predictable in their behavior. This is not, in and of itself, an unreasonable expectation. Nor is it unreasonable to expect employees to read and understand certain information that is relevant to their work. Hospital management further believes that an unacceptably large number of employees fail to meet these requirements. Clearly, this is a problem in search of a solution.

What is important for this study, however, is that management believes literacy training is the vehicle to develop these expected behaviors in its employees: Employees will be transformed if they become more literate. In other words, for management, literacy is more than reading, writing, and speaking well. Rather, management holds a whole set of beliefs about literacy's power to transform individuals into workers who are silent, obedient, and easily controlled — more fully acculturated into the work environment management wishes to maintain.

MARGARET'S STORY: "Making new people"

Margaret is also convinced of literacy's power to transform workers, and the guidance she provides the center about the project is grounded in her beliefs about work, literacy, and advancement. Table 2.2 summarizes those beliefs.

The Open System

Margaret assumes that the workplace is basically open for advancement to anyone who possesses solid basic skills. She believes that many employees are capable of moving up in that system, but they don't realize their potential or how to go about developing it. As Margaret explains, the goal of the King program ought to be to give the "at-risk population an awareness of their potential to move up in the system." If they improve their literacy skills, she reasons, they can "make it":

> They've never thought of themselves as people who have a lot of potential. Um, there's, there's a mind-set that says, "I'm a good person. I work hard. I'm a good worker." But there's nothin' there that says, "And I could be right up there at the top if I wanted to be."

Table 2.2.   Margaret's Beliefs About Literacy Training,
             Workers, and the Workplace

Workplace	Open for individual advancement
	A good place to teach job-related skills, but not "social skills"
Workers	Have the desire and potential to advance at work
	See individual advancement as a primary measure of success
	Have not learned basic skills in school
	Role of worker separate from role as community member
Literacy training	A change agent
	Not taught well in schools
	Can and should be taught at work
	A value-neutral process
	Should meet employer's needs
	Is separate from "social skills"
	Should be tied directly to job tasks

> But people, I think, need to be consciously aware that they have a
> lot of options and they have potential no matter how old they are,
> what sex they are, what race they are [inaudible] you know to go
> up as far as they want to go.

Margaret's view of workplace literacy training as a means of fulfilling
"potential" is based on the belief that the system offers options to those
whose intelligence and literacy skills are adequate. Another more tacit
assumption is that low-level employees want to move up and are blocked
by their own lack of literacy skills from doing so.

Margaret is aware of the potential for "gatekeeping" — setting up
barriers to keep people out of jobs — but she doesn't indicate that it is a
pervasive activity in the workplace, and she doesn't want to contribute
to gatekeeping in her own work. "I don't want to go down as a gatekeep-
er," she explains. Instead, she thinks of enhancing literacy skills on the
job as a way to help others realize their potential for advancement.
Improving job performance by improving basic skills is directly tied to
"making it" in the system.

Like management, Margaret believes in a causal link between acceptable levels of literacy, job performance, and job advancement. Literacy is the missing link in a chain of success and opportunity for both

employer and employee. Margaret does not, in her early presentations, suggest that there might be other reasons for employees not advancing at work. Thus, employees that Margaret describes as being "stuck in grunt-level jobs" are stuck there at least in part because they do not have literacy skills or an understanding of their own potential to move up in the system.

The Portable Toolbox

In her first presentation, Margaret explains that employee performance is best improved by the acquisition of a set of skills that can be adapted to fit any number of jobs. She describes this as the "portable toolbox" of basic information-processing skills. It is not job-specific training, but a set of metacognitive skills that will increase employees' ability to perform a variety of different jobs. In this way, employees will be taught the strategies to become flexible workers:

> Not just content stuff. They had content in junior high, they had content in senior high. Then they got out to work in the real world and none of that stuff looked like what they had been doing, so they avoided it — cause they were never very good at it, cause they didn't like it to begin with. And if we give them more of it, it won't help much.

Thus, as Margaret explains it, employees need the ability to break the process away from the content of the job.

Decontextualization and metacognitive awareness are central to Margaret's method of developing the portable toolbox. She explains that all processes can be reduced to a discrete set of basic skills that are embedded in all work tasks. These basic skills are ways of processing information characterized by linearity, sequence, and separation, what Strickland (1990) has called a conception that portrays the individual as unitary, constant, and rational: "relatively unconstrained by sociohistoric forces" (p. 293).

Margaret argues that if a worker has this set of skills, then he or she can be employed in a complex and rapidly changing job market. What a 16-year-old high school dropout learns working in a warehouse can, she explains, be used for a better job in the post office. Therefore, when Karen and Aisha develop the curriculum for the literacy project from the actual work scenarios of the employees, Margaret encourages them to look for the underlying processes that drive the tasks. The written text involved in the job becomes a vehicle for implementing these processes rather than only something to be comprehended.

Margaret believes that this training will produce workers who will, as a result of their literacy skills, support the current system in the hospital. She describes this as "working it through the system." In supporting the system, workers will reproduce its knowledge, adapt to its transformations, and advance its goals. Margaret does not discuss whether this approach might have political implications. Instead, she presents the portable toolbox of basic skills as a value-neutral set of abilities having little to do with what she calls the "social stuff."

Margaret is careful to distinguish between the teaching of the skills she believes are embedded in jobs and the teaching of broader social or personal skills. For example, "Dishonesty is something employers identify as a critical area, but that's probably something we can't teach in lessons." When Karen presses her on the matter, she explains:

> You can build in skills about how to communicate to your supervisor without getting fired, but that's tricky stuff to do in the amount of time you have. Maybe you want to layer it subtly so that 75 percent is literacy stuff and 25 percent is something else.

The "something else" is not social or personal skills so much as the "employability skills" that employers value. She suggests, for example, that oral communication skills can be taught if they transform employees' communication to more closely match employers' expectations: "Learning how to give feedback or receive feedback or know that it's inappropriate when they get it, knowing what to do with it."

In general, Margaret is concerned with teaching the skills employers want their employees to have. Workers' personal literacy goals and Karen and Aisha's analysis of what employees might need to learn are secondary to employer needs. Moreover, because an outside funding agency is paying for the training, it is also important to meet the guidelines set forth in the grant proposal. In addition to meeting employer goals, the center is obligated to provide the kind of literacy training the funding agency wants. This moves the entire process another step back from the immediacy of the employees and their needs.

For example, when Margaret comes for a visit in the middle of the project and finds the curriculum "not tied tightly enough to job tasks," she expresses concern that the center is not meeting the requirements of the funding agency. She wants the curriculum "tightened up" to get it "back in line" with the initial goals of the grant. As she reminds them, "I know why they put the money on the street."

When Karen observes and interviews employees she concurs with Mr. Lewis, the kitchen manager, that they are often single parents in need of additional child rearing skills. She thinks that if employees learn management skills in class they can then apply these skills when dealing with children and other personal situations. Margaret, however, reminds her that the only way those needs can be addressed is indirectly, as a result of learning job-related literacy and then being flexible enough to apply it to other situations. Thus, the responsibility for change other than improved productivity is placed squarely on the individual. Family and child-rearing issues are separate from workplace literacy skills and are not to be incorporated in the curriculum. This belief in the separation of job literacy skills from personal and social literacy needs is one point of disjuncture between Margaret's approach to literacy and that of the ALRC staff and the hospital employees who participate in the project.

After Karen and Aisha identify the problems management believes are caused by a lack in basic skills, they perform a literacy audit similar to the one mentioned in the introductory chapter. Publications such as *The Bottom Line* (1988) suggest that a literacy audit will yield a "detailed picture of job-specific basic skills requirements and should result in training that doesn't waste time or money in non-relevant areas" (p. 13). The context in which the literacy events are situated is ignored. The goal of this approach is to meet employer needs rather than worker needs, and to meet those needs quickly.

Reading to Do

As suggested earlier, this literacy audit symbolically represents popular beliefs about knowledge and knowing — an epistemological, ontological, and ethical stance. It rests on the assumption that knowledge is objective and measurable and that all trained observers will see the same sets of skills embedded in a particular job task. When they do not, it is because they are missing something or they simply lack the ability needed to perform the audit. Margaret explains, for example, that it is difficult to learn to do a literacy audit, and only four out of ten people have the skills to do one.

At King Memorial, Karen initially identifies the skills as the kind of "reading to do" tasks described by Diehl and Mikulecky (1980). This behavior consists of either reading with no learning or reading with only incidental learning. The authors maintain that it makes up approximately 63 percent of all work-related reading. It tends to be important but not vital to the performance of the task, and it is usually done on a daily basis. The kind of text varies from small chunks of text to other visual displays such as charts and graphs. Table 2.3 reviews the kinds of reading and other literacy skills identified as important to teach the employees at King Memorial. These skills reflect the needs of management. That is, they are the skills needed to make a worker more efficient, less likely to rely on oral communication, and more predictable in behavior. The skills are designed to transform the worker into the ideal employee. They are not geared to developing a more critical and independent individual. Rather, the kinds of skills to be taught are meant to develop a controlled and uniform acquisition and display of knowledge.

After Karen and Aisha identify skills to be taught, they begin to develop instructional units to teach or, in the workplace literacy jargon, "deliver" the skills. Margaret explains that these instructional units should be very tightly organized and must "hook right back into the job task," so that an outside evaluator can look at the lessons and "know exactly what is going on."

I have already argued that conceiving of jobs as consisting of processes that can be measured, described, mutually agreed upon, and then taught to those who do not yet have them is reminiscent of the factory model of learning. Margaret reflects this model in her stories of "cranking out curriculum," of "twirking it around" to make it "fit" funding agency regulations, in her admonitions to "tighten up" and "get things back in line." Job tasks are conceived in assembly-line detail: The employee begins with one step and then goes on to another, moving from

Table 2.3:   Literacy Skills Believed Necessary to Perform
             Effectively

Skill	Specific Process
Reading/writing	Following directions
	Sequencing tasks
	Accuracy
	Locating items
	Recording information
	Matching
	Comparing/contrasting
	Using text to acquire and display knowledge
	Formalizing knowledge display
Mathematics	Rounding up/down
	Estimating time/weight
Oral communication	Learning appropriate ways to communicate with superiors

the beginning to the end of the task one segment at a time. Underlying these steps is a process or set of tools used to manufacture knowledge.

As a result of this skills enhancement, the hospital employees are to become more efficient in the performance of their jobs and hence more promotable. This, in turn, will lead to an enhanced self-concept. Personal needs will be met by way of employment needs being more fully realized. The hope is that workers will see that what they are learning has relevance beyond their jobs. Learning literacy at work will thus help the hospital primarily, but might also transfer into other areas of the employees' lives as well, developing self-esteem and creating initiative for more education and advancement.

Thus, the King Memorial project is initially grounded in the belief that what is good for the employer is good for the employee—to be more productive and flexible, to define self in terms of work, and to seek advancement in the system. And if employees see personal value in this training, Margaret hopes that some of them will seek further education on their own time. What this story does not include is the possibility that employees might perceive their literacy needs differently—that they might believe that what is good for their employers is exploitive of them, or that the system might not be as open as Margaret believes it to be. In addition, the project's definition of workplace literacy tends to set up boundaries about knowledge and knowing. As we shall see, by privileging sequential, linear, decontextualized knowledge and interaction with written text, the program risks alienating employees whose beliefs about their own literacy needs and their own ways of making knowledge differ dramatically from the beliefs of those who develop the curriculum.

Thus, the King Memorial program reflects the beliefs about literacy problems and solutions expressed in the literature and in the funding agency's Request for Proposals (RFP) much more than it expresses those of the persons actually involved in the project. The tension between the funding agency's requirements and the goals and expectations of the workers begin to escalate as the program is implemented.

STORIES IN CONFLICT: Karen and Aisha

The classes begin in January. Each class meets twice a week for 90 minutes. Classes last for six-week sessions, although employees can enter or leave the program at any time during a session. Employees are released from work to attend. Before I actually enter the classroom I attend a training session for tutors, where I hear Karen and Aisha describe the program and the employees and explain what is expected of the tutors. Their discourse at this meeting is a preview of future conflicts—deep-seated conflict over their respective interpretations of theory and practice, subtle conflict over power relationships, and open conflict over defining the problem and the solutions that emerge from their definitions. The conflicts that take shape in this initial meeting will grow over the next several months and eventually undercut the cohesion of the project.

Theory and Practice:
"All our assumptions . . . were shot down"

The most apparent tension arises over the extent to which Karen can integrate theories of text with the reality of practice. She attempts to do this in her opening remarks to the tutors:

> There is a distinction between workplace literacy and regular literacy. The first thing we do is a literacy audit. Through interviews and observations we identify certain jobs we want to target for curriculum development. Then we interview and observe the workers and the supervisors, gleaning the literacy skills inherent in the job. From this audit we develop the curriculum that draws from the literacy tasks required and performed in the workplace. This process derives from whole language theory. Thus the literacy performance is both contextualized—it grows out of the natural environment—and integrated. That is, reading, writing, numeracy, and oral skills are all combined in job simulations. . . . Whole language was first developed to teach young children to read. We're not teaching skills but performance . . . teaching literacy skills through real-world activity.

At first Karen sounds quite comfortable with the theoretical approach she is describing for the tutors. She suggests that there is no real difference between whole language and functional context approaches to defining literacy. As I suggested in Chapter 1, however, real differences do exist in many interpretations of these two approaches. Karen, in a mix of whole language and functional context, defines the context *not* as the language of the individual learner but as the job he or she performs—as Karen or Aisha observe it. Within this definition, curriculum is not developed from the individual worker's unique language, but by a literacy audit that systematizes the worker's language and behaviors as they are perceived by the auditor. An employee's description of and his or her performance of a specific job is thus objective: It can be observed, described, and measured. The concept of authentic language (and, I would argue, by extension, authentic cognitive processes), which is central to whole language instruction, is co-opted by an observer's description of literate performance.

After Karen explains the process of performing a literacy audit and developing a curriculum from that audit, however, she continues in a different direction:

> When we entered the workplace all of our assumptions about the setting and the workers were shot down. Based on the literature we thought that people would be dissatisfied with their jobs, they would perform poorly, and they wouldn't stay long. But what we found was the opposite. People were stable and didn't leave their jobs, people were happy with their jobs, and people performed their jobs well. We also found the jobs we targeted were literacy-proofed and that the problems were actually oral communication. . . . The upshot is that we had to make changes in our planned curriculum when most of our expectations were shot down, so now our tack is . . .

At this point, Karen reveals a frustration with the process of conducting a literacy audit based on assumptions drawn from a literature review and a series of interviews with management. When she begins to talk to employees and front-line supervisors, a very different picture emerges — one that suggests that the literacy audit is not as helpful as the literature suggests it will be. Karen is concerned that the real problem is not the performance of job tasks but poor oral communication skills. She is frustrated to find that her survey of the literature and her interviews with management have produced knowledge at odds with what she observes in the workplace. What she discovers is that although employees can perform tasks fairly well, they appear to be unable to talk about them the way she has expected. Chapters 4 and 5 deal with this disjuncture in more detail. For now, it is important to consider that conflicts over competing theories of literacy instruction as well as conflict between theory and practice make the initial stages of the project quite difficult for Karen. As the project unfolds, these initial conflicts are complicated by other conflicts, especially those Karen and Noreen will have with Aisha.

Goals in Conflict: "What is the bottom line?"

In any program designed to enhance literacy, someone or something gains some power. Noreen, the ALRC director, believes that this is not necessarily a zero-sum game: For workers to gain the power of enhanced literacy, it is not necessary for someone else to lose power. During the tutoring session, Aisha asks Noreen whose needs should be met in the program, and Noreen gives a fairly balanced response:

> *Aisha:* Should the classes be task-specific? . . . What is the bottom line for measuring success?
>
> *Noreen:* The focus is on individual enhancement primarily and then on improved functioning in the hospital. The funding agency will want to focus on the individual and the workplace. The final report should focus on both.

More than anyone else at the center, Noreen sees the project as a balancing act between what the funding agency wants and what she personally believes is appropriate. Although her personal politics place her in sympathy with the employees, her professional politics require that she spend most of her time securing grant money to keep the center afloat. The delivery of services to the employees at King Memorial is only part of a larger commitment Noreen has to basic and applied literacy research. Thus, extending the power of institutions (hospital, university, and funding agency) is of necessity as important as educating the employees at the hospital.

Karen and Aisha, however, focus their energies on either extreme of Noreen's middle-of-the-road position. Karen is scheduled to be reviewed for promotion and tenure, and the portion of the project she is most interested in includes meeting the goals of the university and the funding agency. At this point in her career, establishing a successful track record of attracting external funding is more important than delivering services. If she does not earn tenure, she will have no further opportunities to deliver services through the university. In addition, the center's mission is to conduct research and evaluation rather than to provide literacy instruction. So for Karen, the actual teaching of classes is of less importance than the research component of the project. Karen's concern is focused on the institutions involved in the project, and understandably so. These institutions hold the most power over her professional success. Aisha, on the other hand, is not involved in advancing an academic career and is thus much more focused on the delivery of services to members of what she considers her own community. For Aisha, the empowerment of the workers is her primary concern, even at the expense of the institutions involved in the project.

As a result, Karen and Aisha have quite different goals. These differences are exacerbated by the unequal distribution of power held by the two women. At first, Aisha avoids a confrontation over the issue of power by placing herself in a dependent role. For example, in the tutor training session described above, she portrays herself this way:

> I don't see myself as a teacher but as a person with a strong sense of the Black community. I am learning from Karen and Noreen how to craft workplace literacy and everyday life. They bring this up [in class] every day. I get a chance to learn. Noreen and Karen interpret everything for me.

Indeed, although Aisha has had more contact with the employees and supervisors than either Karen or Noreen, and it is Aisha who has written the letters to the tutors inviting them to the training sessions, it is Karen who does most of the talking in the meeting. Aisha keeps much of her story quiet and presents herself as dependent on Karen and Noreen for guidance. When she does speak up, she is more concerned with the needs of the employees than with the requirements of the grant.

Aisha claims her power in more subtle ways. She attempts to control her time and space, for example, in ways that disturb Noreen especially. Following university requirements, Noreen hires Aisha as a staff person to work eight hours a day five days a week. Noreen expects Aisha to be at the hospital or at the center for those eight hours each day. Aisha, however, thinks of the day as something to fill with as many activities as possible. Remaining in an empty office late on a Friday afternoon seems to her to be a waste of time. She does not see it as her job to answer the phone, and she often is not there to do it. She resents the institutional control of her time and the fact that the faculty members at the center have more flexible work arrangements. Karen, for example, who is released to the center only part time, is rarely there a full eight hours in any given day. She has other faculty duties, and she is also able to work at home if necessary. Aisha takes offense at this difference from the beginning, but she is quiet about it. Instead she claims her time by scheduling it heavily with commitments other than working at the center. As Karen, Noreen, and Rose are to discover, behind Aisha's rather quiet facade is a shrewd social activist with strong personal goals for herself and for the program.

Problems and Solutions: "Through a narrow keyhole"

A final conflict in the project concerns the conditions that contribute to the employees' lack of literacy skills. As Karen and Aisha describe the employees, two contradicting patterns emerge. Karen suggests that the employees are deficient and Aisha suggests that they are victims of oppression. Karen considers deficit theories to be reductive and problematic, but she tends, in her talk about the employees, to frame their use of language in just such terms, even though in the same meeting she describes these same employees as both competent and stable. (See Hull, Rose, Fraser & Castellano, 1991, for a discussion of how deficit theory still subtly shapes notions of underprepared learners.) Moreover, Karen seeks psychological explanations for these "problems." Not only are employees deficient, but they deny they are deficient, which makes them less reliable and more difficult to transform. Karen puts it this way:

> The goal of the curriculum is formalizing. Their communication is disorganized. They need to formalize, develop steps, work in a formal situation. . . . The cycle of the target population seems to be one of compensation and denial. . . . The supervisors are seeing the newer employees as more restless while the older ones are more stable. The supervisors are finding it increasingly more difficult to find stable people.

Part of Karen's tendency to characterize employees as deficient may be the result of her spending more time with the literature and the managers than with the employees. The other part is possibly the result of being confronted with a difference that does not fit into her schema for how people display knowledge. Without other categories of thought to describe what employees actually do, Karen concludes that she is observing deficient skills and behaviors.

Aisha, who spends most of her time with the employees, also characterizes them as lacking in certain skills: "They have a lot of misinformation. . . . A common problem is mispronunciation." But she blames this on a lack of *access* to skills rather attributing it to a lack of ability or to choice. For Aisha, employees are undereducated because of their social and economic circumstances which are in turn a result of their ethnicity. She believes that their lack of literacy skills is the result of an oppressive system that has denied them access to the education needed to speak and write standard English and to think critically about their own positions in the system.

As a result of their different interpretations of what the problem actually is, Aisha and Karen come up with different solutions. Karen develops curriculum that focuses on developing basic print-literacy skills tied to job tasks and texts. Aisha, as we shall see in a later chapter, focuses on using a wide variety of reading materials and writing assignments as vehicles for developing critical thinking and self-esteem. Rather than casting the problem in psychological terms, Aisha casts it in social and economic terms.

As a result, Aisha feels conflict between the requirements of the grant, which Noreen and Karen expect her to honor, and what she perceives to be the needs of disenfranchised members of her own community. As she tells me after the meeting, "They [Margaret, Karen, Noreen and Rose] look at literacy through a narrow keyhole when right next to them is an open door they cannot even see." Aisha believes that the project's focus is too narrow, and she tries to open the project up to new interpretations, new models. As she explains in the training session:

> The workers have come with their own personal agendas which are very important and motivating. . . . Our partnership is not just with King Memorial. We must bond the class. . . . We are helping them negotiate their day-to-day lives. We need to make this an experience and not just an empty exercise.

Aisha thinks that dealing with job-related skills "can quickly become an empty exercise." She finds the lessons dry and uninteresting. Teaching Karen's job-related curriculum becomes a thorny issue for much of the program.

As we shall see in Chapter 5, this conflict is extended by each woman's beliefs about the functions of text. For Aisha, text describes a starting point, an opportunity for creating or improvising a variety of possibilities. For Karen, Noreen, Rose, Margaret, hospital management, and the funding agency, text prescribes a rather specific reality. Each of these men and women have been trained to be more focused on text than on action. Text holds very serious meaning for them. They consider it a given, for example, that one creates and follows lesson plans to teach skills.

For Aisha, text is a story that contains hidden stories. She does not worry that what the literature describes and what she learns at the hospital are two different things. In fact, she is not even surprised. It simply confirms her strong belief that one cannot trust everything one reads.

EMPLOYEES' VOICES: "I wish I could say what I want"

When I begin attending classes, I want to listen to the employees, but at first most of them seem very quiet and reserved. Some of the younger women in the classes are rather outspoken in informal conversations and do not seem uncomfortable answering Aisha's questions or contributing to the lessons. But for the most part, employees wait expectantly for Aisha's directions. On my first day as a tutor, I notice how nervous some of the employees seem to be. When I work with Mr. Fletcher, helping him list a particular procedure in steps, his hands shake as he carefully writes his answers. He says very little to me in the process, choosing to focus on forming well-shaped letters instead. Ms. Benson, another employee, talks to me in such a soft voice that I can barely hear her. In the corner next to the window sits Mr. Stone with his arms folded firmly over his chest, avoiding contact with anyone else in the room by looking blankly out the window.

(I notice in this first meeting that Aisha calls employees younger than her by their first names and those who are older by their last names. Aisha explains that this is a tradition in the Black community — a sign of respect. I adopt this naming convention as well.)

After a few class sessions, I begin to think of the employees as silent, and I think that I understand why Karen describes them as such "poor communicators." As soon as I develop this notion, however, I have to readjust it to fit a new series of classroom events. On the final day of the first session, Aisha asks the learners to evaluate the program. She does not hand out forms, but rather encourages them to talk with her about what they want from her and from the classes. She opens a floodgate of stories and responses. The class, which has seemed so silent and defensive, comes alive with discussion. The conversation does not follow an IRE pattern; instead, there is significant overlapping and co-speaking. I am unable to audiotape this conversation, but I am able to take detailed notes. I am also given a glimpse of why the employees have been so hard for me to hear.

It starts when Geraldine arrives in class with the reddest, longest fingernails I have ever seen. Forgetting my researcher role, I blurt out, "Are those real?" Geraldine shakes her head no in a very quiet and private way. Later, she explains that she doesn't mind if I know, but she doesn't want any of her coworkers to find out. This is to become an important theme — being quiet for protection. Employees are quiet in class at first because they do not trust one another. They are also quiet at first because they do not trust me. And when they do speak, I do what they expect me to do — I hear deficiencies in their language and their thinking processes that lead me to believe that they have poor thinking and oral communication skills.

But this day of evaluation changes all that. First I hear several workers compliment the program. Mr. Fletcher says "[the program] helped me knock the rust off my brain and thinking like doing research and homework. I like to write new things down and learn new words — the meaning of words." Mr. Nixon comments, "you [Aisha] are nice and straightforward. You made us feel at ease. . . . You took some pins out of us. The quiz questions you gave us. They was good just to get my scruples going." Then Ms. Leslie says two things that startle me. First she confesses that she liked being chosen for the classes — a surprise since participation is supposed to be voluntary. Next she says she really wants to work on her GED. This is, in some ways, even more surprising, because the classes are supposed to avoid any GED or pre-GED training. I wonder where she has gotten that idea.

But the most surprising voice belongs to Brenda, who works in the kitchen. She starts up slowly, but gains momentum and is soon talking so quickly that I must strain to understand her.

> I get depressed because I don't make no money. It adds burdens. I got big ideas, that's my problem. That's the way I think. I don't feel like I belong where I am. I'm not afraid of leaving. I'm not in love with King at all. At first I didn't like what you did. I've been through it all. The problem is you get branded in a certain role and they won't let you get no other jobs.

Then the entire atmosphere of the room changes. Geraldine gets in on the conversation too and the two of them really get going. Geraldine exclaims, "the way peoples get promoted comes from who you know." Brenda adds, "we don't get the cooperation from the supervisors you do. You get a different picture of leadership. They're not interested in us." Ms. Kelly says she admires Brenda's ability to express her thoughts: "I can write it, but I can't speak it." Brenda, meantime, continues on almost nonstop: "They make it so hard. They don't understand that experience goes farther than a piece of paper. I'm tired of throwing dough. Everybody got some skill. Peoples are qualified, they just don't get no opportunity." Geraldine chimes in with an "I know that's right." Ms. Kelly, who has been nodding and "yes lording" during Brenda's talk says, "I wish I could speak up like you, but all I can do is cry and pray." Geraldine says she knows how to speak up because "I got that from my mama."

At that very moment, Noreen arrives to distribute certificates of participation from Bayside University to each of the workers in the class. Her arrival lulls the storm and people settle back into more quiet roles. But they are excited about the certificates. Geraldine smiles at me when she receives hers and mentions her boyfriend, "Boy won't his face be tight," she quips.

Brenda's story and the ensuing conversations open my ears to new stories, situations I do not know enough about, feelings and desires I have not yet heard expressed. I become more interested in talking with the workers outside of class about how they see themselves and their jobs. The silence I have witnessed in the classes takes on a new dimension of frustration and anger. Throughout this episode, Mr. Stone sits with his arms folded, looking out the window.

The next chapter moves further into the social and historical context of Bayside and King Memorial to explore the significance of Ms. Kelly's tears and prayers, Brenda's outrage, and Mr. Stone's silence.

CHAPTER 3

Seeing Ghosts

King Memorial Hospital is both old, in the sense of tradition and social structure, and new, in the sense of development and transformation. By adopting and exploring a group of metaphors the hospital employees themselves use, this chapter moves beyond tears, prayers, outrage, and silence to consider how and why they (the Others) interpret the institution as reproducing social relations in the antebellum past, thus inviting a continuation of traditional patterns of resistance. Although the political economy of the region has changed in the last century, the players in this drama are haunted by these ghostly relations even as they attempt to exorcise them.

The History of King Memorial Hospital

In the years immediately following the Civil War, a "New South" began to emerge from an agrarian past. Southern orators, journalists, and politicians aggressively encouraged Northern industrialists to move the South's cheap labor off the land and into the factories. In addition to courting development from outside, Bayside's politicians organized many efforts to modernize on a more local level. One of their most successful projects was a subscription campaign to raise funds for a general hospital to serve what was then termed the "indigent sick" of Bayside and the surrounding area. In January of 1892 King Memorial Hospital admitted its first patients.

Actually, King Memorial was two hospitals, the White and what was then called the Colored. This physical bifurcation is a powerful symbol of the racial and class segregation that was to continue both in the hospital and in the city itself until the 1960s. It continues today in the separation of hospital staff along class as well as racial lines. It can also be interpreted as symbolic of the definitions of literacy that separate those who are credentialed from those who are not, those who take on middle-class values from those who do not, and those who are willing and able to advance at work from those who are not.

Eventually, the original separation in the hospital and the city healed into a visible scar, an ever-present reminder of racial, social, and institutional stratification. For the poor urban Black community, the hospital has been and still is "the Kings"—a linguistic reminder of both two separate hospitals and the separation many poor Blacks still experience daily. For the middle-class Black and White communities, however, the naming convention has long since become "King"—perhaps an effort to silence the naming of separation, an effort to make it invisible. This theme of separation will surface again as we examine in the next section the various ways employees, academics, and governmental funding agencies make meaning.

Since 1921, King Memorial has had a working agreement with nearby Delta Medical College, a private, elite institution. Currently it is a major teaching hospital housed in a building 21 stories high with a floor-space area of 24 acres. The hospital holds 1,200 adult and child beds and 350 bassinets in its nurseries. There are 23 elevators, 18 surgical operating rooms, 24 emergency rooms, 15 delivery rooms, and 27 x-ray rooms. The outpatient clinics are housed in a separate wing that is seven stories high.

Recently the hospital has experienced a financial strain that is becoming more and more unbearable. Supported primarily by the county, it is constantly seeking more funding. Many King Memorial supporters think that the state should pick up more of the financial burden. Spiraling health care costs combined with the unwillingness of local taxpayers to shoulder any more of what they see as an unfair burden have put the hospital in a particularly vulnerable position.

A View from the Outside

In late October, I begin regular visits to King Memorial and am immediately struck by how different it is from the private uptown hospitals. In fact, to me it seems a world, or at least a subculture, unto itself. The first people I pass each day are those who seem to be perpetually on the street outside the entrance to the building—and outside mainstream society as well—the drunks, the drug addicts, the 13-year-old mothers, the vagrants. In a kind of bas relief I also see the young, starched-white nurses, doctors, and students busily learning the art of healing in a place that is a perpetual open wound.

Inside King Memorial, it is crowded and busy. The elevators are slow and always jammed with an unpredictable mix of wellness and despair, but they are much preferred to the stairwells, in which more than one person has been mugged, raped, or even murdered. The police officers who are stationed on the pediatric floor to protect children injured in drug wars usually wear flak jackets. During the project a young patient is shot twice by an unidentified assailant while in one of the elevators (the newspaper accounts speculate that it is over a cocaine deal). Like many other public institutions, King Memorial has its share of scandal as well as danger. One day Aisha tells me that two lab technicians have been let go because they were caught blackmailing a coworker. The victim paid them off by check, kept the canceled stubs as evidence, and recently turned them in. Aisha laughs at the madness of it all, and especially at the blackmailers' foolish willingness to take their pay-offs in the form of checks.

The local belief is that King Memorial is by far the best place to go if you are in an automobile accident or have been raped, cut, or shot — it has an excellent emergency room. But it is a terrible place to go if you are sick. Essentially King Memorial is a place of extremes — the best and the worst of public health care. The insurance claims made against the hospital have become so high that the state legislature recently declared the hospital immune from prosecution, and it is no longer possible to sue King Memorial for medical malpractice.

There is a certain irony about King Memorial's very existence. It was originally founded as a hospital to serve the indigent sick in the region. However, it also serves as a teaching hospital. In serving the poor, it also provides service for the privileged — a place to learn their trade. Many of them graduate, settle in Bayside, and go into private practice. They remember King Memorial as a place they are happy not to see or think about. One former nurse, now married to a successful surgeon who served his residency at King Memorial, tells me it is "the kind of place that is so needy it will eat you alive." She claims that her friends who still work there have no other life — they have become completely enveloped in the suffering and despair that are a part of the hospital's everyday fare.

For me, as a White, middle-class, academically trained woman with no experience in health care, the intensity of the hospital evokes images from "M.A.S.H.," "St. Elsewhere," or a Dickens novel. But the employees who work as entry-level staff in the hospital see a very different set of images.

Mythical Realities: The Ideology of the Plantation

One way to begin to understand a group's underlying categories of organization is to examine its metaphors. As I listen to the metaphors of the employees who cook the food, wash the linen, and do the cleaning at King Memorial, I hear talk of slavery and bondage, struggle and freedom, getting out and being free at last. And as they speak, I sometimes see in their eyes the legacies of slavery and the shadows of an earlier oppression.

It is Mr. Stone who first suggests to me that the structure of the plantation might help explain employees' beliefs about their positions within the structure of the hospital. Like many others, he often complains bitterly about his supervisor. On one occasion, he describes how she has told him that he makes too much money:

> Talking 'bout we making too much money. I say, "Where? How can you make too much money?" I make five dollar an' eighty-six cent an hour and she say that too much. She just work to harass peoples, that's all. She enjoy that. She got a bunch of slaves. I'd keep them, too, if I had a bunch of slaves like that, too, all I had to do was order them around. They follow instructions good. Got one of them don't want to follow instructions, that's me. I don't want to follow no crazy advice. There time for everything, and it time to be treated right.

Aisha names King Memorial the "Last Great Plantation" shortly after she starts working on the literacy project, and she maintains throughout that the supervisors act like slave drivers. One day early in the first six-week session she tells me that she is meeting with the heads of housekeeping, food service, and laundry to work out "the overseer problem" — the problem of employees not being allowed to attend classes because they have too much work to do. Even Rose suggests that the music to accompany a video made by ALRC about its project at King Memorial should be "Tara's Theme."

There are some very specific reasons why employees at King Memorial often evoke plantation metaphors when describing their jobs and their social relations at the hospital. These reasons are bound up in employees' perceptions of their work as physically difficult and often demeaning, their supervisors as sometimes mean and hateful, and the hospital in general as being totally dependent on their work yet virtually unconcerned with their well-being. In short, the employees believe they have been assigned slave-like status in the hospital social structure.

These images of slave-master relationships suggest a time when the South was structured around the ideal, if not the reality, of the White male father holding absolute authority over all White women as well as all slaves. This ideology supported the economic and social relations in the antebellum South. The plantation was a powerful symbol of organization and held sway over the entire culture, even though only a small portion of the White population ever lived on a plantation or owned slaves. This social structure gave White men, as the house "holders," ultimate authority and kept all others at home. The effects were far-reaching — on politics, law, the economy, and social relations. In order to understand these effects, let us shift our gaze to the times before the Civil War, when elite Southern men put their "ladies" on pedestals and their "darkies" in the fields and the kitchens.

Patriarchy, Love, and Control:
"He loves them because they are his"

The assumption that the White male was "the apex of power in the antebellum South" (Leslie, 1988, p. 20) was maintained by defining Southern White women as "weak, dependent, illogical, and pure" (p. 19) and slaves as little more than savage brutes to be domesticated into service for the common good. The goal of "civilization" in the plantation ideology was for the elite White male, at the expense of White women and slaves, to accumulate property and to enjoy leisure and the arts. As William Harper wrote in his "Memoir on Slavery" in 1853, "[I]t is better that a part should be fully and highly cultivated, and the rest utterly ignorant" (p. 32). Harper recognized that within a society organized around the institution of slavery "a large class of society is cut off from the hope of improvement of knowledge" and that for these beings "blows are not degrading." He defends this position with the rhetorical question, "But why not, if it produces the greatest aggregate of good?" (p. 50). Hierarchy, slavery, and the subjugation of women were thus justified because they produced the most civilized society (Leslie, 1988).

Other apologists for slavery argued that it was a necessary evil and that it was the best way to ensure the perpetuation of Christian values: "Christian morality . . . was not preached to a free competitive society, but to a slave society, where it is neither very difficult or unnatural to practice it," wrote George Fitzhugh in *Cannibals All! Or Slaves Without Masters* (1960, p. 205). In this defense of plantation ideology, God was the ultimate patriarch, and his manifestation on earth was in the master-slave relationship. The master is unequaled in power, all others in society are his property, and thus all others depend on him for their existence (Leslie, 1988). Or to use Fitzhugh's words, "Slavery, marriage, [and] religion are all pillars of the social forces" (pp. 205–206).

An issue of considerable debate began in the late 1960s. It centered on the notion that not only had White males internalized this ideology of oppression as the justification for their privilege, but White women and Blacks had done so as well. Bartlett and Cambor (1974), for example, have suggested that these ideals "played a powerful role in shaping the behavior and identity of southern men and women of the planter class before and after the Civil War" (p. 10). Several psychoanalysts, including Elkins (1968) and Hunter and Babcock (1967), have argued that slaves might have internalized the childlike dependency ascribed to them by Southern ideology. Historians such as Genovese (1967) and Lewis (1967), on the other hand, have argued that although slaves might have been perceived as childlike in the dominant culture, they developed a "fuller personality" in their own subculture (p. 18). The internalization of some aspects of their purported childlike behavior by White women is fairly well accepted in the literature (Bartlett & Cambor, 1974; Greenacre, 1947; Fox-Genovese, 1988; Leslie, 1988; Scott, 1970), but the suggestion that slaves also internalized childlike identities has been much more openly questioned because of their maintenance of separate communities, apart from the master's.

More recently, Ogbu and Matute-Bianchi (1986) have argued that internalized oppression is a kind of thinking typical of "caste-like minorities":

> Minorities . . . have become incorporated into a society more or less involuntarily and permanently through slavery, conquest, or colonization and then relegated to menial status. (p. 90)

They further maintain that one of the most important qualities of these minorities is their exploitation by the dominant culture and their response to this exploitation by internalizing the discrimination and coming to believe that they cannot succeed in the same ways as the middle-class majority. As a result, they have developed a set of survival strategies that include "norms, values, and attitudes as well as competencies or skills that may not be congruent with striving for school success" (p. 93). For the purposes of this study, it is important to recognize this issue as important, but not fully resolved.

In either case, the ideal system of paternalism and hierarchy was an orderly, closed system based on loyalty, love, and obedience. In reality, of course, antebellum life was marked by acts of disloyalty, brutality, and resistance. Just how deeply these realities permeated the lives of slaves and their masters is also important to consider.

Forms of Resistance

Within the ideology of paternalism and hierarchy, and enhanced by it, was a strong sense of community among the slaves. Their West African heritage emphasized family ties and traditions passed on in story and song (Graff, 1987). Slavery, by its very nature, may have strengthened these bonds. For example, Fox-Genovese (1988) maintains that slave women worked hard at creating and maintaining their communities:

> Slave women worked as many as eighteen hours a day. Their regular relations with the other men, women, and children was grounded in that work — in the skill of performing it well, in the fellowship of performing it together, in the determination to establish and define its limits, and, when the master's work was over, in the love of beginning all over again for the Black family or members of the slave community. And slave women demonstrably resisted the worst effects of slavery, resisted it at the very core of their identities . . . they resisted slavery as members of a community, as well as in lonely defiance. Their multiple contributions to the culture and communities of their people constituted a web of resistance that sought, above all, to protect the identities and cohesiveness of members of succeeding generations. (pp. 33–34)

Slave resistance was manifested in varied forms according to the specific context that provoked the actions as well as the immediate goals. The most obvious were the slave revolts organized and led primarily by Black men. These were committed at the deepest levels of resistance, and the consequences were the most severe.

In addition there were persistent incidents of resistance that were carried out on a daily basis in order to protect and ensure the survival of the community as well as the individual (see Table 3.1). All these forms of resistance had one thing in common: They were overt acts by slaves to regain or maintain some control over their lives within a social structure that afforded them very little control over anything. Interestingly enough, although some of the more overt and violent acts such as arson and murder were obvious rebellious acts, many other, more common forms of resistance took place without the master's full awareness. In-

Table 3.1.   Forms of Slave Resistance and Motivations

Motivation	Resistant Act
Control of time	Shirking work Hiding out
Control of material goods	Taking Hiding
Control of space/body	Infanticide Abortion Self-mutilation Running away
Control of language	Sassing Defying Special language Clandestine literacy
Control of life	Murder Suicide

stead, the slaves' actions were interpreted by the master as signs of indolence, ignorance, or poor moral character. The master then used this interpretation to justify his total authority to "care for" those who were unable to care for themselves.

The most common forms of resistance were initiated to gain control over time. Slaves often shirked difficult or unreasonable work by pretending not to hear or understand the verbal instructions of their masters. In more extreme cases, they ran away temporarily to avoid work. This kind of temporary running was more common to women, perhaps because they were punished less severely than men, or because they were less willing to be separated from their families and children (Fox-Genovese, 1988).

Slaves also resisted their oppression by taking goods from the master. They did not necessarily consider this stealing, but rather appropriating goods that rightfully belonged to them. The master, on the other hand, tended to see the act as stealing and was more likely to associate it with moral weakness. Terborg-Penn (1987) suggests this difference in beliefs about ownership had roots in the differences in the structures of African and Anglo-American communities. She describes African communities as much more inclusive and egalitarian than the Western model of individualism and opposition. Material goods in the African community were conceived of as ours, but in the plantation community they were conceived of as his.

The slave woman, realizing that the master also thought of her body as his, sometimes resisted his efforts to use her body to reproduce labor capital and then separate her from it. She denied the master access to the commodity called her children by sexual abstinence, abortion, and sometimes infanticide (Steady, 1987). The master was often unaware of these measures because it was not uncommon for slave and White babies alike to die from a variety of illnesses (Fox-Genovese, 1988).

Some women even prevented separation from family and children by making themselves useless on the auction block. Fox-Genovese (1988) tells of one woman who chopped off her right hand and threw it in the face of her master to prevent him from selling her away from her children. The forced separation of families and especially of mothers from children was rooted in the ideology that slaves were property to be looked after rather than humans beings with their own knowledge, abilities, and beliefs. Slaves in turn resisted these definitions with every means they had available. From dramatic uprisings to everyday accidents, slaves worked steadily to undermine the authority of the master.

Slaves also used language as a form of resistance. Not only were there commonplace incidents of sassing and defiance, but also the development of Black English. Baldwin (1988) argues that slaves developed a special kind of language not because they were unable to learn standard English, but to protect themselves from the oppression of the master. He maintains that Black English is a result of the diaspora. Slaves were unable to speak to one another because they came from many different tribes. They were joined together by their lives as slaves and the church they developed under the watchful eyes of the master.

> It is within this unprecedented tabernacle [the early Black church] that [B]lack English began to be formed. This was not merely, as in the European example, the adoption of a foreign tongue, but an alchemy that transformed ancient elements into a new language: language comes into existence by means of brutal necessity and the rules of the language are dictated by what the language must convey. (p. 164)

Baldwin argues that this language was developed so that slaves could communicate with one another in a way that the master could not understand. Their very language, Baldwin asserts, was an act of resistance against White dominant culture. But this act of resistance was interpreted as a sign of ignorance, an inability to use language "correctly," a sign of cognitive deficit. This tradition of defining linguistic and cultural difference as a sign of racial inferiority helped justify and perpetuate slavery, and slaves' persistent resistance to oppression served to reinforce the master's perceptions of them as helpless and childlike — in need of his perpetual protection.

The plantation master knew the power of using the word as well as the power of speaking "proper," so by 1820 it was illegal to educate slaves. It was generally believed that literacy would teach them to despise their work (Leslie, 1990). The punishments for learning to read and write were often severe — cutting off fingers, whipping, branding, or selling the offender away from family and friends (Graff, 1987). These were the consequences of literacy for Black slaves in the South until 1866. Despite these monumental barriers to any sort of literacy, however, fully 5 percent of the slave population was literate (Graff, 1987).

Slaves deeply valued education, and when they were emancipated, they believed that it would gain them the rights and rewards of first-class citizenship. For a few brief years this promise was almost realized, but by the late 1870s, Blacks in the South had lost their civil rights, the control of their labor power, and their hope of decent public education (Anderson, 1988; Graff, 1987). Instead, Blacks were provided an education fitting their assigned station in life as the lowest of the working class (Anderson, 1988).

Throughout the nineteenth and well into the twentieth century, Southern Whites continued their oppression of Blacks through legal means, and Blacks continued to resist this oppression in whatever ways open to them. The story of their oppression and their resistance does not stop with the Emancipation Proclamation, but continues up until the civil rights movement and beyond. Indeed, in this study, poor and working-class Blacks resisted control in ways that Whites often interpreted as incompetence, laziness, or moral weakness. Today, however, the labor commodity defined by the needs of the dominant class is not physical work but functional literacy and competence with standard English. Jordan (1990) has suggested that these definitions of competence require African-Americans to either hide their Black English or give it up. She argues that this denial or loss has resulted in a destruction of the systems of knowledge indigenous to the African-American community and to individual identity as well.

She goes on to explain that Black English is associated with a "pre-technocratic culture" that places little value on abstraction. As she points out, there is no passive voice in Black English. There is a need instead to make clear the agent who commits the action in a sentence. She calls this a person-centered value that assumes two real people at work in any exchange of language. As we shall see in Chapters 4 and 5, the presence of real live people in the production and consumption of text has important implications for the ways in which workers display (or disguise) their literate behaviors.

Historical Metaphors: The Hospital as Plantation

Just as ideologies of patriarchy and acts of resistance framed life in the antebellum South, hierarchical styles of management and worker resistance inform everyday life at King Memorial. This can be seen and heard most clearly as workers describe their relations with their supervisors and with one another and their strategies for "gettin' on" in what mainstream culture thinks of as dead-end jobs.

Paternalism/Maternalism: "Sometimes they treat you like a child"

In conceiving of entry-level workers as lacking in literacy skills, management assumes the role of protective parent. Karen describes the supervisors as frequently casting themselves in the role of "critical parent." She records several instances of supervisors describing employees as "childish" and of having "rebellious episodes." Supervisors, in discussing their problems with Amanda, describe themselves as concerned with favoritism and developing "consistency" in dealing with "sibling rivalry." Management often refers to employees as childlike, and employees know of and resent this treatment; they are aware of the role management has assigned them. Some accept the role, but others resist it. Looking back, we can see this theme in one of the stories that opens this study (Prologue, Story 2): "On the job, they treat you like you are a child and talk to you any kind of way." Management, however, does not appear to be aware of the extent to which employees both believe they are being treated like children and find that treatment so offensive.

Nevertheless, although many employees consider this treatment insulting and resist it in a variety of ways, others participate (either for convenience or from conviction) in these relations, which perhaps helps explain why so many employees spend a lifetime working at the same jobs in the hospital. Many of the women who work in housekeeping, for example, appear to take on the helplessness and dependency of children in relationship to their supervisors. Aisha often remarks that they act "like girls." These women tend to seek out, compete for, and enjoy the approval of their supervisors. These behaviors seem to shape an important part of their sense of self-esteem. When asked to write about her best day at work, one employee writes, "When I do a good job and Ms. Jackson said she is proud of me then that is a good day." Other employees tell of supervisors "sweet as they can be" who fill out forms and file papers for them so they will not have to do it for themselves. Ms. Edwards's supervisor fills out the necessary forms for her to go to the clinic or to report an accident. Many other employees describe similar relationships with their supervisors and believe that the supervisors are doing this for their benefit rather than as a way to perpetuate their dependence. They often describe themselves as members of a big family network. As one woman writes in an essay at the beginning of the program:

> My best day at work was when I got my transfer to Strong Hall. It has been a joy working with the people here. Getting to know the students gives me a happy feeling. I work with a good group of people. We are a big happy family.

For example, the women who work under Ms. Butler treat her as if she is their mother or a favorite aunt. When something goes wrong on Ms. Butler's day off, they call her at home to tell her about it. Ms. Butler refers to her female employees as "my girls" even though they are all well past adolescence. Although most of the women seem not to mind this maternalism, it angers some others. It angers Aisha as well. She finally becomes annoyed enough to say something to Ms. Butler. Later, she shares the story in a staff meeting:

> They call Ms. Butler at home even when she is not there. They act like girls. Some of it is education under oppression — internalized oppression. You are always a girl, even if your hair is beautifully grey. Some of it is maternalism. Ms. Butler calls Ms. Fortune "girl" even though she has been grown a long time. I say to her, "Ms. Butler, don't you think Ms. Fortune is a little old to be called 'girl'?"

Aisha believes the women who work for Ms. Butler have internalized her maternalism and thus also see themselves as girls, but Mr. Stone suggests another reason for their behavior:

> They're afraid of their jobs, see. That's their problem. They're afraid and they won't do no better. Let her do anything she wants to do to them. They say, "OK, OK, OK." I can't do that. I can't. I don't know about them. I just can't. I just have to speak up, which uh, the ladies, they don't do, they really don't.

My own data confirm both views. Some women act childlike out of fear or expediency to protect their jobs. Others, however, truly believe that they cannot make decisions or act independently without a supervisor, teacher, husband, boyfriend, minister, or God directing their actions and beliefs. They see themselves as passive recipients of life rather than active agents.

In either case, conceiving of employees as children (and employees reinforcing these notions by their actions) serves to reproduce the hierarchy and maintain control in the hospital. It also helps support the belief that the employees are incompetent because they are so childlike and, because they are so childlike, they must be treated like children. This also serves as a justification for the static nature of the system. Those on the bottom tend to stay there because they are defined as incapable of handling more demanding jobs — jobs requiring adult behavior.

Hierarchy

Like plantation ideology, King Memorial's hierarchy is composed of a complex process of separation and segmentation, with power increasing in inverse proportion to the number of persons in each level of power. It works in much the same way as the plantation model worked — keeping control in the hands of the master.

Hospital administrators in other regions of the country, however, maintain that this particular structure is not limited to the South. Hospitals have long been characterized in general as very hierarchical, with both knowledge and power concentrated in the hands of top management (Boss, 1990; Cohen, 1991). Certainly the plantation is not the only metaphor one might use to describe the power relations at King Memorial. A top-down organization could also be interpreted as an example of the scientific or industrial model described in Chapter 1. But the employees do not use any manufacturing or even behavioristic metaphors in describing their work or their relationships with management. Instead they most often talk in terms of being treated like slaves, and they also talk of being treated like animals or like children.

King Memorial is directed by a White male from the "good ole boy" network of Bayside and staffed by highly educated and specialized physicians. There is a clear dividing line between the doctors and the rest of the staff that cares for patients. Nurses have a great deal of authority — much of it real but unofficial. There is another clear division between the staff that delivers care to the patients and the support staff — those whose work it is to cook, clean, and wash. These positions — the invisible positions that pay not much more than minimum wage — are also the dead-end positions. Their boundedness reflects the Southern ideal of "place" discussed above: One has a certain station in life and stays there—it is, after all, part of God's order in the world.

The Enclosed System

The three areas whose employees participate in this study—housekeeping, food service, and laundry—encompass the work that slaves, servants, and women have done throughout history. Of these three areas, the laundry is by far the most enclosed. Run by Mr. Julius, a young, college-educated African-American, it is housed in a separate building, and the workers there have few dealings with other parts of the hospital. Management sees it as a separate and rather mysterious place. The only laundry employee who has any dealings with the hospital is the man who drives the delivery truck full of fresh linens to the hospital each evening and exchanges them for the soiled ones to be washed, ironed, sorted, and folded for another day's use.

Management describes the laundry as taking care of all its own business from within. For example, Mr. Julius was handpicked for his job by his predecessor, a man who had been in charge of the laundry for years, rather than by hospital management. And when the hospital wants to hire a new driver to deliver the linens to the hospital, no one in the laundry wants the job. Management concludes that no one has a driver's license, but another possible explanation is that none of them wants to leave what is essentially their domain. Given ultimate control of their own territory and labor, they are either unwilling or afraid to give it up. Very few of the employees from the laundry attend the literacy classes. Those who do come for only short periods of time, and their average education level and years on the job are the highest of the three groups.

When Ms. Thompson first came to the hospital she worked in the laundry before being transferred to the kitchen where she has worked for several years. In class she tells how she still misses her friends in the laundry, and if there is ever an opening, she claims she will go back in a minute. She remembers with pleasure the way the work is performed there, and she enjoys sharing her knowledge in class, since the other employees do not know much more about the laundry than ALRC staff does.

The kitchen is in some ways a more open place. It is located on the first floor of the hospital, so the men and women who work there are not separated physically from the rest of the hospital. In addition, many of the women work on the food line, serving meals to employees and visitors. The manager of food service is Mr. Lewis, a middle-aged White man who has worked his way up in the ranks. Many front-line workers see him as no more educated that they are, and they resent his ascent to power. Linda, a young woman who works in the kitchen, speaks out in class one day and claims that Mr. Lewis does not have a high school diploma or an equivalency degree. Two or three other women who work in the kitchen hear her comment and agree with her. Karen and Aisha are also told by two of Mr. Lewis's college-trained assistant managers that he needs as much help with his literacy skills as the employees do.

Mr. Lewis tends to keep a tight reign on the women who work for him. They resist his control with silence and anger. He thinks they are unable to communicate or solve problems; they think he is arbitrary and dictatorial. When the literacy classes start, the employees are supposed to be given the choice of attending or not. As we saw in Chapter 2, however, Mr. Lewis decides who can come from his department, without asking whether they are interested. After the first six-week session, he chooses who has to withdraw and who can remain. When I ask Ms. Collins, one of the women who works in the kitchen, why she has chosen to take the literacy classes, she explains:

> Well, really, I didn't know we was supposed to be havin' no classes. Mr. Lewis call each four us into his office and told us that he had recommended us for this here program that they was havin'. And no one inform us how long the class would last — nothing like that. He just told us that he had recommended us four girls for the business and I was one of the four girls that was chosen. He recommended us and so we came.

Ms. Collins's compliance, and her reference to herself and her coworkers as "girls," reproduces the supervisor's concept of employees as childlike and in need of direction.

In the summer, a new woman from the kitchen starts coming to class. She is making rapid progress and wants to continue, but Mr. Lewis tells her she cannot miss any more work. Aisha is out of town, so the woman begs Rose to intercede for her. But we never see her in class again. The anger and frustration this kind of management evokes can be seen in the sullen faces of the women who work in the kitchen and the explosive arguments they often get into. One employee tells me, "They got lots a problems in food service. Grown womens fighting on the line. They really got terrible problems."

Another day Ms. Benson, a kitchen employee, comes to class with a terrible headache, her whole face frozen in a mask of pain. While Mr.

Stone takes the stairs up to the fifth floor two at a time to find some aspirin, she tells us how her supervisor in the kitchen has shouted at her and "cursed so loud the whole hospital could hear." It upsets her enormously, and she feels like her head is about to "split wide open."

To a certain extent, this kind of treatment and the corresponding employee behavior defines the housekeeping unit as well. The manager, Mr. Parrott, is an African-American man that few of the employees like. During the course of the study, several women in housekeeping tell me about attractive female employees being promoted to supervisor in exchange for sexual favors rather than for their managerial talents. Another employee adds to this portrait of Mr. Parrott by observing during a tutoring session: "We hoped he'd be fired when they arrested him on that second DUI. He spent the night in jail and all, but they didn't." A housekeeping aide complains to me about how rude and arrogant he is to her whenever he comes into the dormitory where she works. The general consensus among the housekeeping staff is, as one employee explains, that Mr. Parrott acts like the "overseer."

I do not know whether Mr. Parrott actually uses sex as a possible method of earning a promotion, and I am not asserting that it is either true or false. But it is significant in two ways. First, it is a very insulting story, told to diminish Mr. Parrott (and the women purportedly involved with him) on a personal and moral level. Second, it is a pervasive story; it is repeated over and over again. The content of the story as well as its recurrence suggest not that the story is true, but how little respect the employees have for Mr. Parrott (and certain supervisors as well).

Furthermore, it suggests that for these workers, advancement can be earned in ways other than job performance or skills enhancement. Other comments during the course of the study confirm this belief. When talk in class drifts to earning a promotion, several employees tell Aisha, "It's not what you know, it's who you know." Each employee has a story to tell of someone else who got the job—not someone more skilled, but someone with the right connections or the right politics. To suggest to employees that a lack of skills is keeping them from advancing is to risk appearing naive about how they believe the culture at the hospital is actually organized.

It could be argued, perhaps, that employees tell these pejorative stories on all their supervisors because they do not like anyone in charge of them, but this is not the case. Many employees are genuinely fond of their supervisors. Furthermore, the relations between employees and supervisors are not driven by race or gender. For example, Mr. Richards, who works as Mr. Parrott's assistant, is a Black man that everyone is quite fond of. I never hear one negative rumor about him, but several employees do tell me they like him because he is fair and honest. Amanda reports that all the women in the supervisors' class like him very much. She also finds him particularly pleasant and cooperative. He is especially helpful to Aisha when she needs to negotiate time for employees to come to class or address problems they are having with their floor supervisors. He does not remain at King Memorial for long, however. At the end of the project, he is transferred to another job outside King.

Ms. Edwards tells me that she used to have a supervisor she was quite fond of, "a White lady who treated us so nice. . . . She talk to us so nice it make you want to do just anything for her." Ms. Edwards describes some of the supervisors as "just as sweet as they can be" but others are downright "hateful." Mr. Stone feels the same way. He works for two supervisors, both of them White women. Although he has a very hard time getting along with Ms. Butler, he is especially fond of the head nurse in charge of the emergency room where he works most of his overtime shifts. Overall, employees determine whether or not they like a supervisor by the way he or she treats them, and especially how the supervisors speak to them, rather than because of the supervisor's race or gender. As Mr. Stone tells me, "But I think color shouldn't matter . . . I don't care . . . as long as they respect us."

Another housekeeping aide writes with frustration about why she attends the literacy classes. She explains what she wants:

> A better paying job without so much hard work. When you are working in housekeeping, it is really not a clean job at all, but you are treated just like maybe you was just as dirty. I realize that every job I do or have done is important whether you are treated that way or not.

As several other women discuss in class one day, if they all stop scrubbing the floors, washing the sheets, and baking the biscuits, the hospital will shut down immediately. This realization of the hospital's reliance on their work is juxtaposed against the reality of their positions as invisible workers.

Another housekeeping aide also expresses frustration and hostility over the way he is treated. He tells me, for example, that one of the supervisors wants the housekeeping staff to eat lunch in the basement of the building:

> Don't even want us to, uh, she can sit at the desk and eat. You not supposed to. And then she don't even want us to sit in that little room over there at the tables and eat. She want us to go down in

the basement. Told her, "I'm no dog. I'm not going down in no basement." Before I go in the basement I'll leave. Go to the restaurant somewhere to eat. I'm not eating in no basement. We have places upstairs to eat. She don't want us to eat nowhere. She want us to eat outside like the animals.

Physical Labor: "I'm so tired I don't know what to do"

Most of the entry-level work in housekeeping, food service, and the laundry is of a physical nature. In the laundry the linens are dried, pressed, folded, and returned to the hospital. There exists the constant threat of being burned in one of the pressers, inhaling germs from the soiled sheets, or being stuck by a contaminated needle caught in the folds of the bedclothes. The laundry also has a sewing room where all the uniforms are made. The seamstresses joke about how fastidious the doctors are and how difficult it is to please them in the fitting of their jackets, especially if the doctors gain a little weight.

In the kitchen, the work is also hot, especially in the summertime. Most of the jobs require long hours of standing to prepare food. A typical day in the area might find women chopping heads of cabbage for cole slaw, leaning over a sink peeling dozens of hard-boiled eggs, frying huge pans of chicken, or coming in at four in the morning to bake stacks of cakes and pies. The risks of being burned or cut are ever-present in these jobs. Some of the kitchen workers also describe their work as boring, requiring no thought. As Ms. Collins explains it:

> Once I learned the base — the whole basis of the thing, backwards and forwards and left and right, your mind goes to a blank. You already know what's on the next day. You know how much of this goes in how much of that. You know you don't need no recipes for to do the same thing over and over that you doing day-by-day. And see, your mind gets to where it's just there. It's not functioning.

Housekeeping work includes changing linens, scrubbing bathrooms, mopping, and emptying trash (women's work) as well as the heavier floor work such as stripping and waxing floors (men's work). Housekeeping employees are also responsible for disposing of toxic waste such as syringes and other refuse in special "red bags," which are then burned in the hospital incinerator. Cleanliness is a major concern in the hospital, and employees are expected to clean carefully.

King has a high number of patients with AIDS as well as other more easily transmitted diseases such as tuberculosis. And many of the housekeeping aides are afraid of what they might catch from patients. One day Ms. Edwards puts on protective clothing (as an extra precaution, not as part of hospital policy) to clean the room of an AIDS patient, and the doctor in the room makes her leave and take the protective clothing off. "You might upset the patient," she is told. Ms. Edwards tells this story in class to illustrate the point Mr. Stone has made earlier: that no one at the hospital cares about the health and safety of the housekeeping staff. Ms. Edwards knows that the hospital has told the housekeeping staff that they will not contract AIDS from cleaning a room, but she is not convinced they are telling her the truth.

So even though their work is physically demanding and often quite dangerous as well, employees believe that the hospital cares little for their physical well-being. They perform these jobs with little hope for either a promotion or a raise, and are told they can do no better without the proper literacy skills and credentials. This serves to convince some employees that they are trapped in a static system. It also reinforces and is reinforced by the employees' feelings of oppression and powerlessness.

Illiteracy as a Justification for Control

As previously discussed, in the antebellum South, it was common ideology that slaves were in their positions because they could do no better, and this justified the master's complete control, taking care of them as part of his property. In a somewhat similar manner, the management at King Memorial sees its entry-level staff as incapable of functioning other than on the most rudimentary of levels. Management does not discuss the possibility that employees' behavior might reflect their anger over their lack of power and control. But instead of attributing incompetence to race, as the slave owners did, current management links this perceived incompetence to a lack of literacy skills and credentials, differences that express a strong class division.

It also justifies the lack of advancement that decent jobs would provide. Just as plantation ideology supported stasis, the labor economy of the hospital strains toward entropy. Management tells Karen and Aisha that most of the employees in entry-level jobs are older and more stable workers, but they also tell them that the employees are confused and lack the skills necessary to handle anything more than entry-level jobs. The majority of employees who come to the literacy classes have been in the same jobs since they were hired, many for more than ten years. Although some employees appear satisfied in these jobs and perhaps even believe that they can do no better, others see themselves as competent and dream of a promotion. But beliefs about language, literacy, and competence create credentialing requirements that tend to keep them in entry-level jobs despite their desire for advancement.

Resistance

Employees in the hospital, like those on the plantation, resist their employer's attempts to control in a variety of subtle, often undiscernible ways. Just as the master might not think the cook intentionally burned the biscuits as an act of resistance, the hospital management seems unaware of the acts of everyday resistance in which its entry-level employees engage. Some of these are explicit acts, and employees willingly talk about them with pride. In fact, they find them to be quite amusing. These acts are not carried out with the grim seriousness of political correctness, but with the playful humor of those who know an uproariously funny joke but must conceal it from public knowledge. This form of resistance gives employees a sense of agency they lack in their institutionally imposed identity as workers. Other acts of resistance appear to be more tacit. An almost automatic set of responses to new and strange situations are the sudden silences and blank expressions that employees often use when Aisha asks them to do something different in class or when someone new enrolls in class. They do not trust new people or new ways of doing things, and they mask this mistrust with a veil of silence as a protective barrier from real or imagined danger. When workers respond this way outside of class, middle-class managers (both Black and White) will often conclude that the employee is lacking in literacy skills and that training will lead to new behaviors that will solve the problem.

But there is another possible interpretation. Instead of signs of illiteracy, these behaviors are often forms of everyday resistance against work that is perceived as unfair — a set of survival skills to adapt to being perpetually on the bottom. Table 3.2 summarizes specific behaviors that

Table 3.2. Employee Behaviors and Interpretations

Behavior	As Deficit	As Resistance
Not following directions	Inability to think sequentially	Anger Power struggles
Not planning ahead	Inability to think critically	Anger Power struggles
Not talking	Poor communication skills	Hiding out Anger

management and supervisors often complain about. It shows how these behaviors can be interpreted as signs of two very different problems.

In the first interpretation, the behaviors are taken as a lack of basic literacy skills; in the second interpretation, the behaviors are taken as signs of resistance. The King program is justified by the first interpretation, but this assumption proves to be problematic. Although management assure ALRC staff that employees lack the literacy skills to perform their jobs with competence, employees do not see themselves as unable to perform their work. Rather, they see their work setting as exploitive and have developed subtle forms of resistance to this perceived exploitation. As a result, employees understand curriculum that focuses on learning to improve current job performance as insulting. This is not to suggest that the workers in the classes do not want to become better readers and writers, but they do not tie this to a deficiency in the ways they perform their work and thus want to learn new things — things that have little to do with sweeping, cooking, and washing.

For example, the behavior of some of the women who work the line in food service does not suggest to the supervisors that these employees are involved in a power struggle, but rather leads them to conclude that these women have no critical thinking skills. During the summer, one of the managers complains that they are always running out of cut lemons on the line because the woman in charge of stocking the line is unable to think ahead and make sure there is a backup of lemons to replenish the serving container before it becomes completely empty. Supervisors make similar claims about the way the milk dispenser is allowed to become completely empty before it is refilled.

In another instance, Mr. Lewis tells Rose that he has assigned an employee to keep the various items stocked on the salad bar. The employee does what Mr. Lewis tells him to do for a few days, but then seems to forget that things need to be filled up. Mr. Lewis concludes that the employee has difficulty with memory and problem-solving skills.

But this behavior is actually one way for employees to claim some power and control at work. It is an understandable consequence of a work setting in which employees feel exploited. As Aisha explains in a staff meeting:

But these same women would get the milk at home. See at work, in the cafeteria, their lips are all pushed out . . . think about the power struggle. Fighting is their way of claiming authority. They choose not to do it. It's a fight. When I go to the cafeteria and they are standing there with their arms folded, they're in a fight and I

just walk on by cause I know I'm not gonna get my cold plate today.

Employees confirm this interpretation as well. They talk of fighting in
the kitchen quite a bit. They claim that many of their coworkers stay
mad all the time about one thing or another. They are often angry when
they came to class and complain about their supervisors and their jobs
frequently. They tell me with great relish of other acts of resistance. For
example, when the county inspectors comes to perform the annual hospital evaluation, there is a screen missing from one of the windows in
the kitchen. An employee has removed it because she believes the screen
blocks her only source of fresh air. Mr. Lewis takes great pains, after the
failed inspection, to find and replace the screen and then lectures the
kitchen workers on the importance of the screens always being in place.
The employees' discomfort in a miserably hot kitchen in the summer
heat is not addressed. Mr. Lewis does not consider it — the employees
don't mention it. The next time the inspector comes around, the screen
is gone again.

At about the same time chicken is burned in the ovens then carefully placed on the patients' trays and sent up to the floors for dinner. In
both of these instances, which occur in the same week, managers are
frustrated and angry, but they do not consider that these events both
happen immediately after heavy physical demands are placed on employees while preparing for the annual inspection. Instead, the supervisors see this as more proof that the kitchen employees are unable to think
critically.

But in class each day, the employees are talking about how hard it is
to prepare for an inspection, how much more work they have to do, and
how little appreciation they receive for the extra work they perform.
Many employees miss class during inspection week, and others come
only to fall asleep. Ms. Collins tells me that she has been on her feet
from 7:00 AM to 1:30 PM without a break "even to go to the restroom"
and she is "just worn out."

At this point in the study, I begin to suspect that literacy is not
really the problem at all. Indeed, of the various players in the kitchen
drama, those who appear the least able to think critically, the least able
to read the text in its broader definition, are those supervisors and
managers who do not consider the possibility of employee resistance to
apparently unreasonable work demands during the preparation for the
hospital inspection.

I see this theme repeated in housekeeping. Here the employees have
worked out their own ways of dealing with the work demands they
consider unfair and the supervisors they dislike. Sometimes they are

obviously resistant, but at other times they are outwardly cooperative—resisting in more subtle ways.

For example, when Ms. Edwards is assigned to a new supervisor, she tells me that her coworkers dislike the new woman so much that they get together each day and plan what they are going to do to make the woman's job as difficult as possible. One of their favorite solutions has to do with literacy. They do not tell her anything, such as how they do the schedules or other job specifics, but "let her look it up in the book instead." They intentionally act both docile and dumb in an effort to make the supervisor suffer, but in a way that will not get them into any trouble.

Eventually, however, the supervisor retaliates when she assigns Ms. Edwards to work weekends, which Ms. Edwards has not had to do in the whole six years she has been at the hospital. Ms. Edwards switches from resistance to outright rebellion at this point, and simply tells her supervisor she is not going to do it. When the supervisor insists, Ms. Edwards goes to the assistant manager. Ms. Edwards describes their meeting:

> And he was fixing to take my side when she up and told him about all the money it would save the hospital and his eyes got about this big [making a circle the size of a plum with the index finger and thumb of each hand].

After Ms. Edwards comes in to work on her first Sunday morning, she is so tired she calls in sick the next day (for the first time in six years). The supervisor then tells her she needs a doctor's excuse for being out sick on a Monday. Ms. Edwards tells her supervisor that this is against the rules and she is not about to pay a doctor $60 to tell her she is tired. The battle continues between these two women until the supervisor is fired for falsifying time sheets, perhaps her own act of resistance.

Mr. Stone uses subtle and overt forms of resistance with Ms. Butler. He refuses to talk to her when he is angry over something she has done. He ignores her as much as he can get by with, knowing it irritates her more than anything else he can do. Once they get into an argument because, in his opinion, she does not give the male employees any "respect." Rather, he thinks she caters to and protects the "ladies." He tells her so, and she becomes very angry. Then, in Mr. Stone's words:

> That's why I quit talking to her. "How come you don't talk to me?"
> I told her, "I ain't got nothing to say to you. You're wastin' my
> time." I'm not gonna waste my time talking to her when it don't do
> no good. I speak to her and go ahead and [inaudible]. I don't hate

her, but I don't like the things she do. What she do, she don't do it right. She don't do it equal.

Other employees turn to more destructive forms of resistance. Instead of hurting anyone else, they hurt themselves. In addition to having a very high rate of absenteeism, some employees come to work drunk or high on marijuana. They spend their days in a kind of stupor, not talking to much of anyone, performing their jobs with a kind of mechanical compliance, "hiding out" as Aisha says — running away somewhere inside their bodies while they stay to perform their work. They seem to have no interest in advancing in a place where they survive by making themselves as invisible as possible.

When the master on the plantation had to deal with the difficulties of the slaves, his picture of them as ignorant and helpless prevented him from seeing them as resistant to his authority. In a similar manner, the supervisors at the hospital have pictures of the entry-level employees as confused and illiterate, which prevents them from seeing that perhaps many of the employee problems are conscious acts of resistance. In the slave quarters, this was known as "puttin' on ole massah." Today it could be called "puttin' on the manager."

My own experience spending time with employees outside of work is that many of them are very organized and attend carefully to details. My first inkling of a level of problem solving and critical thinking far more complex than management realizes occurs one day when Mr. Stone tells me where he has gotten his watch — the one with all manner of functions. Mr. Stone explains to me that he found it in the parking lot outside the hospital, and he realized that although it was damaged, it could probably be repaired. So he took it to a store that sells those watches and copied the manufacturer's address from one of the watches on display. Then he mailed his found watch back to the company, and for $5 the company sent him a new one. As Mr. Stone tells me the story, I realize that this man, who has been described by his supervisor as a poor worker and whose literacy program pretest scores indicate poor reading skills, is neither confused nor incompetent. Mr. Stone does not have extensive formal schooling, but he certainly has the ability to think critically and to problem solve. At work, however, he is careful to hide his ability from those he does not trust.

After the program is over, Rose and I meet with Ms. Edwards, Mr. Stone, and some others at Aisha's house. They each drive (following written directions) in the middle of a thick Southern thundershower. At the meeting, we talk of the class and what they have been doing since it has ended. At one point they both talk of how careful they have to be about what they say at the hospital because some of their coworkers are too talkative and cannot be trusted. Each of them displays the ability to plan ahead, to follow instructions in adverse conditions, and to analyze people and situations. They acknowledge the need to be quiet and careful to protect themselves from jealous employees and vengeful supervisors.

Gone with the Wind: The Sequel

When I begin this study, I have little experience with workers outside of the university. I have no idea that the ideology of the plantation informs the daily experiences of so many working-class Black men and women in Bayside. When I recognize the frequency with which they use metaphors from that ideology, I realize how important it is to understand not just the contemporary setting that grounds a study, but its historical underpinnings as well.

There are certainly a variety of ways that workers who believe they are oppressed or exploited might talk of their experiences. But in Bayside, the talk about work is often talk about slavery, and the talk about advancement is often talk about "gettin' out." What constrains these workers is not just a rigid hierarchy with little opportunity for advancement, but also the belief that the system is arranged so that one can do no better, that one must remain silent as a form of protection, and that the workplace holds many enemies as well as many friends. These structures and norms of behavior might work against any form of literacy training that might be introduced into the hospital.

For those who have never attended to the lives of the working poor of the South, this ideological remnant is perhaps difficult to imagine. But during the months of this project, I begin to see the ghosts of the past — of slavery and the plantation, of stasis and inequality — roaming the corridors of the hospital, the halls of the university, and the marketplaces of the region. For example, I have lived most of my life in the South, yet until this study, I have never noticed how pervasive "plantation" is as a naming convention. Now I see its ubiquitousness with discomfort. As I work on this book, I vacation on the Gulf of Mexico with my family in a house called "Tara's Dream" in a resort community called simply "the Plantation." On our drive through Georgia, Alabama, and into Mississippi, we pass several "Plantation" gas stations, pecan groves, peach stands, shopping centers, movie theaters, restored homes, and new subdivisions.

Down in the Delta, David Duke attempts a presidential campaign after losing a strong race for the governorship of the state of Louisiana.

A new wave of racism is sweeping the nation even as the white majority shrinks to minority status. Calls to arms against multicultural education surface in the strangest of all arguments — the defense of freedom of speech and the cultural integrity of the country (see Stimpson, 1991, for an excellent analysis of the relationship between multiculturalism, freedom of speech, and academic freedom in American education).

It is not surprising, then, to consider that remnants of resistance accompany remnants of oppressive ideologies in this study, as they might in any other workplace or region with other ideologies of oppression. But using theories of resistance to explain why workers behave in certain ways defined as illiterate does not fully explain their actions or the outcome of the program at the hospital. In order to do that, the next chapter shifts from a sociohistorical perspective to consider epistemological and ontological issues that also contextualize literacy.

CHAPTER 4

Making Connections

In Alice Walker's *The Color Purple* (1982), Celie writes a letter to her sister Nettie describing how Darlene (one of Celie's employees) criticizes Celie's talk, telling her she sounds "confused" or "like a hick." Darlene is trying to teach Celie to talk "proper." Celie tries, in an effort to humor Darlene, but she is far from convinced that talking "proper" will improve her life in any significant way.

Darlene attempts to teach Celie to talk proper by bringing her "a bunch of books. Whitefolks all over them, talking 'bout apples and dogs" (p. 193). Designed for White children rather than Black women, the text and pictures in the book have little importance for Celie. But Darlene continues with her attempts to transform Celie, and Celie continues to both humor Darlene and resist change.

> But I let Darlene worry on. Sometimes I think bout the apples and
> the dogs, sometimes I don't. Look to me like only a fool would want
> you to talk in a way that feel peculiar to your mind. (p. 194)

Celie's struggle with Darlene illustrates the point made earlier (in Chapter 3) by both Baldwin (1988) and Jordan (1990): Blacks who speak and write Black English often encounter barriers in dealing with those (of all ethnicities) who use standard English as a measure of competence. As Darlene explains to Celie: "Colored peoples think you a hick and white peoples be amuse" (p. 193). For those men and women who use Black English at King Memorial, hick translates into incompetent, and supervisors, rather than being amused, are inclined to point out a literacy problem.

Celie also reflects on those things that bring her joy, that make her life full. Relationships, connections with Shug and Nettie and the children, even with the proper talking Darlene and her twin sister Jerene, are what make Celie a happy woman. She has little interest in being "educated" in order to make herself more respectable. She already has what she wants — "love, work, money, friends, and time." What more can any of us ask for? Darlene thinks there is more and causes Celie some slight bit of irritation in her contention that Celie's talk makes her a "dead country give-away" (p. 193).

But there is a deeper issue here, one that Celie describes when her language is continually corrected by the "proper" talking Darlene: "Pretty soon it feel like I can't think. My mind run up on a thought, git confuse, run back and sort of lay down" (p. 193). What Walker is suggesting, I believe, is that in attempting to change people's language, we are tinkering not just with the way they pronounce words, but with the very ways they construct knowledge.

Celie is thinking just fine until she starts to worry about the apples and the dogs in the "Whitefolks'" book, things that have little importance in her world. But when she tries a new way of talking, she "gits confuse." She concludes by reflecting that this is a foolish, senseless thing that will not make her life or her work much better.

In a similar fashion, a functional context approach to workplace literacy is more than an attempt to teach employees to read and write. It is also an attempt to change employees' ways of constructing and displaying knowledge to more closely match those of mainstream employers and educators. The ethical and political dimensions of functional context are not usually addressed in program development, nor is the range of responses employees might have to these attempts to change their ways of knowing. As a result, when ALRC initiates the literacy project at the hospital, no one wonders if the employees might consider its emphasis on linear, sequential knowledge acquisition and display as "feeling peculiar to" their minds, nor does anyone consider that they might resist the program.

In order to understand the extent to which a functional context approach to teaching literacy also becomes a method to change knowledge construction and display, this chapter examines the beliefs about knowledge and literacy that inform this position. This will make it possible to recognize and appreciate the ways in which the employees already construct and display their knowledge and why they think the functional context approach is "for the pits."

Analytical Knowledge

Inherent in the curriculum developed using the literacy audit are several assumptions, which were discussed earlier. As we have seen, most of these assumptions rest on an approach to constructing knowledge that emphasizes abstraction and decontextualization and suggest industrial models of manufacturing products. Job tasks are separated into discrete categories and sequential tasks. Making and communicating meaning is most often achieved by reading and writing text. Emphasis is placed on the objective, quantifiable aspects of a message or a job performance rather than on its context or interpretation. According to Belenky, Clinchy, Goldberger, and Tarule (1986), this kind of knowledge is analytic and requires a separation between the self and what then becomes the object of study. They further suggest in their description of "separate knowing" that analysis appropriates a certain power and distance over the other. As a result, analytic knowing creates the need for resistance because, they argue, it is the kind of knowledge that "invites coercion and withdrawal" (p. 167). This is an important point as we begin to consider why many of the employees in the program actively resist learning based almost exclusively on analytical decontextualization of work. They do not resist only because the lessons are developed by White middle-class women, or simply because the curriculum is an expression of the employer's needs. Rather, they resist because at times it is so different from what they believe knowledge and knowing to be about. In other words, their resistance is not only a political act, but also an individual effort to gain or maintain personal control over their own authentic and effective ways of making knowledge and using language.

In this study, it would be consistent with other research to frame analytical and relational knowledge as a dichotomous opposition divided along lines of gender (as have some feminists such as Belenky et al., 1986; Gilligan, 1982) or ethnicity (as have some educational anthropologists such as Cohen, 1969; Lipka, 1991). But in point of fact, although the differences clearly exist, they are shaped by the program participants' degree of commitment to the hierarchy and power relationships in the institution rather than to any of the categories usually associated with these differences. Moreover, they anchor either end of a continuum rather than posing a set of oppositions. I recognize both kinds of knowledge production used by employees in different situations. And as we shall see in the next section, some employees draw on relational knowledge more than others. But in general there are clear preferences for one kind over another.

Developing an Analytic Curriculum

Karen, the daughter of an academic and trained in an elite university in literary criticism, begins the literacy audit listening for the analytic voice. But, as we heard in Chapter 2, when she goes to interview hospital employees who are deemed competent, she does not always hear it. First she thinks the problem is a lack of oral communication skills. Much later, as she listens more, she concludes that the employees are "involved in some sort of women's ways of knowing, and maybe we can build that into the curriculum." But she finds this difficult to do. Relational knowing is outside the boundaries of what the grant will fund, and the center is responsible for spending the funding agency's money according to the guidelines of the grant.

During the literacy audit, Karen's and Aisha's perceptions of the literacy tasks inherent in the jobs (or lacking in the jobs) overlap in some areas, but are not identical. Karen speaks of the difficulty of having to "translate" Aisha's observations when developing curriculum from tasks she does not observe herself. The difficulty is that Aisha and Karen are hearing and using two different ways of making meaning when they speak with the employees and when they write their own notes.

Karen concludes, after several days she terms "exhausting," that the employees targeted for literacy training are working in a "literacy-proofed environment." As far as she can tell with this initial audit, there are really very few literacy skills required to make cole slaw, mop floors, or wash sheets. The workers perform these tasks, but they do not seem to be able to talk about breaking each task down into steps. Karen sees this as work that is physically demanding, dangerous, and that requires little in the way of thought. Because the employees are not interacting with print, she concludes that they are unable to use print symbols in a meaningful way. She suggests that the employees are people who do "not do much thinking." For Karen, work that is not performed in a print-rich environment seems to be mindless activity. Meaningful symbols are those related to text. As a result, Karen finds developing curriculum from her first observations in the hospital to be quite difficult. But she wants this program to work, so she spends many hours working on lessons that are theoretically sound and that fit the description of the grant proposal she and Noreen have written.

Aisha sees the same behaviors in the interviews she conducts. She is confounded, for example, by the housekeeping aide who cannot explain to her how to empty the Sharpes needle container even though the woman performs the task daily. She concludes, however, that the employees possess a kind of knowledge that is quite different from the sequential ordering of tasks that the project's curriculum is trying to teach. She believes the employees have skills and meaningful symbolic interactions that are not analytical or tied to print literacy.

In Chapter 2, I used Karen's comments to the tutors to illustrate her belief that employees lack a formalized pattern of communication. She establishes as the program's first goal to "formalize" communication that is "disorganized." Workers need to "formalize, develop steps, learn sequencing skills." Karen is describing the analytic knowing that she does not hear clearly when she interviews employees. Analytic knowing is tied very closely to traditional academic education, which centers on the written word. In focusing on this word and privileging it over experience, the center staff is disconnected from the relationships that shape the experience of many persons in the project who are not so dependent on text.

Text-Dependence as Knowing

As Chapter 2 illustrated, hospital management sees written text as an efficient way to communicate information, to ensure uniformity of performance, and to increase productivity. Thus, becoming reliant on text for sending and receiving information is one goal of the literacy program. It is believed that if employees are more reliant on and capable of using text, they will be better, more knowledgeable employees. And this, in turn, will make them promotable to higher positions within King Memorial. Like Margaret, Karen believes that there are basic skills inherent in employees' jobs, and, based on management's claims, she also believes that the employees avoid recognizing them.

Thus, the goal of enhancing skills can be achieved by encouraging employees to focus on text for meaning. This will not only make them more like the "new people" management wants them to be, but will make them more competent in their personal lives as well. Personal competence is measured by reliance on text. Here Karen explains this belief to Rose while they are developing some reading exercises:

Rose: A lot of sequencing they've gotten, but . . .
Karen: It makes you dependent on other's behavior [if you have to rely on others to show you the steps]. We have to look at the discrepancy between "do as I do" and the written-down process or the concept of the process that the higher-ups have of the process. Put *inferencing* under the category of making interpretations of written material. Inferencing is exercising judgment. If they can't do it with text they probably are not doing it in the other areas of their lives.

EMPLOYEE METHODS OF MAKING MEANING:
"Feelin' the rhythm of the day"

Unlike most of the educators in this study, the employees tend to make knowledge and conceive of their world and their work in ways that are much more connected, gestalt-like, and physical. This general

pattern varies across the individuals in the classes. Some of the employees are able to use an analytical approach to making knowledge, and
others rely much more heavily on a relational method. However, in
general, across these individual variations, the preference for relational
knowing is quite strong, especially in comparison to the preferences of
ALRC staff. For example, instead of conceiving of their tasks as a series
of steps, the women in the laundry talk of the need for a rhythm to the
day, a rhythm of taking the sheets out of the dryer and putting them in
the presser, a rhythm of folding and sorting and stacking together, as
members of a group. They express a certain pleasure in performing as
part of an organic unit, establishing a pace and maintaining it through
the course of their work. When one woman takes a break, the rhythm is
adjusted to make up for her absence, but the rhythm continues on
almost uninterrupted.

Not only do the employees express feelings of connection to a team,
they also talk of being connected to their work in ways that develop
harmony rather than distance. They become one with the task. Ms.
Edwards describes her work as a housekeeping aide this way: She enters
a room and cleans it holistically, every task related to every other task
like a cloth without seams. She even has devised a way to use her tools
for more than one purpose so she will not have to carry or reach for so
many. She has difficulty describing what she does in a sequential manner, but suggests that it all happens at once like a well-orchestrated
event rather than a series of tasks linked together linearly.

Ms. Collins gives me a similar description of preparing the wild rice
cold plate that is served in the hospital cafeteria each Thursday. It
includes preparing a marinade into which she places chunks of hot
turkey breast. When the time is right, she adds other ingredients and
arranges the plate with a variety of garnishes. This process takes place
while she is preparing other dishes and waiting her turn to use some of
the equipment necessary for food preparation. All of these things are
done without the use of a timer or a recipe. I ask her how she remembers
it all, and she laughs and tells me it is in her head and she does not have
to stop and think about it at all. She sets herself a certain rhythm for the
day and her tasks emerge from it, all related, all of a piece. She thinks of
the execution of her tasks as a performance rather than as a series of
steps.

Mr. Stone approaches his work in the same way. He firmly believes
that he knows how to perform the tasks required in his job, but he is
unable to give me a sequence of steps to follow so that I can do them
myself. He tells me that he can repair small appliances and cars in the
same way. "I can just look at it and see how it go." But he says that it is

hard for him to follow the printed directions. "They don't make no sense to me." Print is not an aid in knowing, then, but rather a detriment.

I also see this non-linear performance when I visit Mr. Stone's church. During the service there is talking, testifying, singing, speaking in tongues, and praying all happening at once. The overall effect is intense, almost overwhelming. I think at first that the service does not follow a set order. There is no bulletin listing the events, but everyone knows what is going to happen. They know when to sing, but they have no hymnals. They know when to get out their money for the offering, but I cannot predict when the offering is going to be collected. I ask Mr. Stone how the congregation knows when to do the parts of the service, and he tells me they just know it, but he cannot describe it for me. And each time I attend the service, it is somewhat different, shaped by those in attendance and those who "get happy" (speak in tongues, dance, or become physically active in some other personal way during the service).

In general, workers conceive of events as units with many things occurring simultaneously. Time is not broken up into linear, discrete categories, and work is performed as a synchronous event. This concept of work as performance rather than as a series of steps is not limited to only those men and women who perform physical tasks or who have limited formal schooling. The divisions of analytic and relational learners cross the divisions of position at work, ethnicity, gender, and credentials. Aisha, although she can do both if necessary, strongly prefers a relational style of making knowledge. Sarah and Amanda are also capable of thinking either analytically or relationally, but each prefers to use relational thinking except in situations in which the power distribution is unequal. They see the power relationships inherent in institutions as requiring a decontextualization that they are unwilling to foster.

To all three of these women, keeping the lessons tied directly to job tasks is not only politically unacceptable, it is senseless. For them, everything is connected to everything else. They don't just think about workers, they think about people. They aren't just delivering skills, they are building a community of learners, and this community is more important than the job. As a result, Aisha neither develops nor follows the traditional sequential lesson plan. Rather she puts a lesson on the board or produces a handout that she uses to trigger events, acting as a prompt. What unfolds from that point on is determined by individual employee response. She creates an open-ended pattern for each day that is suited to the particular needs and interests of the group. Moreover, these needs and interests are primarily personal and social rather than academic. Aisha starts each class by asking how everyone is, how their families are, what sort of health or caretaking problems they might be

having. She also seeks out and brings to everyone's attention the personal triumphs of the day. She then weaves these into the lessons, referring
back to them when the members of the class are bored or confused
about a skill she is trying to teach. The context is the group of men and
women working together to learn new things. And this context has a
different shape and dynamic each time the workers and Aisha meet to
re-create it.

Aisha is constantly looking for connections and relationships. She
imagines all sorts of new ways to teach literacy and uses many of them in
her classes. She explains that her teaching is a performance. She goes
home at night and studies the script, but when she goes to class the next
day she performs to an audience, to people with feelings and lives
outside of work. Therefore, she always leaves enough space to change
the lesson. She believes that this is how good teaching should be—
shaped by the moment. It is like the difference between playing Bach
and the blues. One is highly organized; the other, although still carefully structured, encourages improvisation.

Margaret tends to devalue this position and deny its legitimacy. She
is critical of lessons that incorporate aspects of community building.
One of Aisha's first lessons deals with writing a response to a performance of *Raisin in the Sun* that the class has watched on public television as a homework assignment. Margaret calls the lesson "shoddy." As a
result, Aisha, like the employees at the hospital, is defined as the Other—deficient and in need of training. Some ALRC staff members describe her as unorganized, not task-oriented enough, not a teacher.

As discussed in Chapter 1, many ALRC staff members use hierarchy and linearity to structure their workplace. They prefer to separate
their work and their time hierarchically. Materials and supplies tend to
be arranged vertically or horizontally into categories with great precision. They spend a great deal of time organizing the project and the
lessons using text—lists, schedules, job-related information, and sources
from "the literature."

To Aisha, the lessons ALC staff members develop are dry and uninteresting. One day she talks to me at length about how frustrated she is
to be perceived as incompetent. "I'd like to see them [Karen, Rose,
Noreen] take over these classes for a while. They'd lose everybody in a
week," she snaps. In many ways Aisha feels neither valued nor respected
for who she is and what she can do. "Have they ever looked at my
resume?" she often wonders aloud.

In the late summer, when the project is suffering from low attendance and low morale, Karen decides that the staff should meet once a

week to discuss lesson plans and problem solve together. During one such meeting, a tutor questions Aisha's methods of writing out her lesson plans. In particular, the tutor does not think Aisha is being specific enough with a particular homework assignment. Aisha has seen the tutor taking notes in class, and one day she steals a look at the tutor's notebook. The comments she reads make her feel betrayed and not trusted. She concludes that the tutor is spying on her performance in class, just like some of the employees who are sent by their supervisors to spy on one another. "Who gave her the authority to do this?" she wonders to me later that day at lunch. At first she is angry, and she taunts:

> She can mess with me up to point and I'll ignore it, but if she really tries to fuck with me I'll take her out in the hall, and she will be able to fill up her whole notebook and probably need a new one.

But then she softens and begins to talk about her frustrations with the project in general. She tells me that for weeks she has gone home and cried at night. Then one of her closest friends reminds her that no matter what Noreen, Karen, and Rose say or do, she is still the one in charge in the classroom, and she can teach what she chooses — what she thinks the employees need and want to learn. We continue to talk a while longer, and then she looks at me with a weary resolution. "That's all right," she explains, "I'll just take it in my hands and let it go. She just hasn't realized yet that we are all sisters."

These beliefs about the underlying connection of all things are evident in the way Aisha views people's ideas and their work. During one staff meeting the subject of academic honesty is raised. Karen tells a story about how her major advisor in graduate school published the work of one of his students as his own. Karen describes this as typical of the hierarchy in the academic community. Aisha, however, challenges that position by observing that she thinks it is funny that anyone would think they own words to begin with. She claims that in her community everyone shares their words: "The point is for the words to be heard, not owned."

For all the White women connected with the project, the Black women's sense of connection to their community is something we can neither completely understand nor fully describe. But in other ways, Aisha tends to reflect her formalized schooling more than her ethnicity. Although in some respects she is at odds with the rest of ALRC staff, in other ways she is at odds with the employees and does not understand what is making some of the lessons difficult to teach.

Praxis: The Meaning in the Doing

The most striking difference between Aisha and the employees is that although both the employees and Aisha conceive of tasks as organic wholes, the employees map meaning onto activity rather than onto words. Thus to "know" something means to do it rather than to list, describe, and talk about it. For Aisha, one can "know" something by talking, reading, or writing about it. This difference between Aisha and the employees comes into particularly sharp focus one day in class in late summer when Aisha is trying to help Ms. Edwards define the word *comprehend* by substituting it into another sentence.

Aisha: So we have to go back to earlier discussions, earlier words. Ms. Edwards's comprehension of how to close this container is excellent. Her comprehension is excellent. That's how I would be using that word. What would I be talking about?

Ms. Edwards: That needle container.

Aisha: That's just the object of our discussion. But listen to this, look at me. Ms. Edwards's comprehension of how to close this box is excellent. She showed us how to do it. She knew what the steps were. She showed us where the slots were, how to close it. She remembered not to close it cause other classes have to use it, do you remember that?

Ms. Edwards: Yes.

Aisha: What was it that you did? What was it you showed us about this particular box. Did you not know how to do it? Or did you know?

Ms. Edwards: Well, I think I did it well.

Aisha: You did it well, and you did it well because you what? You had the information or did you not have the information. Did you have the information?

Ms. Edwards: Well, I had it in my head.

Aisha: So if you had it in your head did it mean you knew it?

Ms. Edwards: By doing it.

Aisha: Did it mean you knew it?

Ms. Edwards: Yes.

Aisha: Um-hum, it meant you comprehended it. Your comprehension, your understanding of closing the lid on this box is far superior to mine. Your comprehension, your understanding of this was excellent. That's really what that word means. Your comprehension, your understanding, your knowledge. And you then told us what to do if we got stuck. Where to go. You knew all the processes unto the process. So comprehension to you means what? Means you what?

Ms. Edwards: It means I demonstrated how to use that needle container.

Aisha: And you demonstrated it because you — do you understand it?

Ms. Edwards: Yes.

Aisha: Yes, it means you are understanding it. Um-hum. What I'm trying to do is get you to focus in on another word that can be used as another word for comprehension. So if you had to say another word for comprehension, what would it be?

Ms. Edwards: Well, um, the job that I did on the needle container, I did it well, very good.

Aisha: You did it very well because you what?

Ms. Edwards: I knew my job.

Aisha: And you know it cause you — what's the word? Understand?

Ms. Edwards: I understand.

Aisha: Um-hum, um-hum, understand.

Ms. Edwards (under her breath to Rose and me): I done understood it three times.

The frustration each woman feels in this incident illustrates the kind of difficulty Aisha often encounters in the literacy classes. Aisha is thinking of the word *comprehend* as an object to be slotted into a sentence. In the beginning of the dialogue, Aisha says that the needle container is an "object" for discussion. Ms. Edwards, on the other hand, is thinking of the act of comprehension as something to be demonstrated through action. She has a hard time answering Aisha's questions because for her, meaning is defined in the act of doing, not in a word that describes the task. Notice that she says she knows it "by doing it." Here we can hear voices of separation and connection in an exchange that is particularly frustrating to both women. Notice, too, that there is no co-speaking or overlapping speech in the exchange. Rather, Aisha adopts a more formal IRE pattern to get Ms. Edwards to say that *comprehend* means understand. We can hear Aisha's separate voice most clearly as she urges Ms. Edwards to analyze the relationship between the two words. Aisha certainly has these skills, but because they are tacit rather than explicit, she is not always able to teach them.

The employees who are engaged in physical activities tend to find the verbal or textual appropriations of their activities alien and often redundant. For them, it makes little sense to try to translate the economy of action into what they consider the redundancy of words. When asked to write stories or explanations of things, they tend to want to make it "short and sweet." This is a folk term used when employees do not want to use more words to describe something or when they resist using the words as an inappropriate way of making meaning.

Another day, Aisha assigns the class a problem-solving scenario to discuss. The employees have some difficulty with the assignment because they do not think problem solving is something one talks about or conceptualizes sequentially so much as it is something one does. Problem solving is action, not words. This is the assignment that is written on the board:

> It is Wednesday afternoon February 15, 1989. You are the team leader or supervisor. Two of your workers are out sick with the flu. The Joint Hospital Commission is arriving in three hours. You have a problem to solve. What is it? List the steps you will take to solve the problem.

Aisha tells the class that this is their problem for the day. She reads the scenario out loud to them and then asks them to talk about the problem. As she sees it, the task is to decide how to cover for the absent workers and get the work done and to then write the solution in step-by-step form. The employees see the task differently, however. Geraldine shrugs her shoulders, sucks her teeth, and observes dryly that people are out all the time: "I don't see how this is no problem." (Geraldine has come to class to learn how to qualify for a job as a security officer. To her, this exercise is a waste of time.)

During Aisha's verbal sparring with Geraldine, Ruby sits looking at the board where the assignment is written for a moment and then asks me if I have any paper. When I offer her some, she tells me, "I really has some, I just don't want to do this." When I look at Mr. Fletcher's paper, I notice that he has written what appears to be two steps. When I ask him if he can break the process into more than two steps, he tries, but it is hard for him — a new way of thinking about something he does regularly as a team leader.

Ms. Thompson also writes down very little. When I ask her to read what she has written, she embellishes each step with a number of details she has not written down — specific information about certain people and tasks — the local knowledge one must have to get anything done, such as who is cooperative, who is a good worker, who you can trust and who you can't. As she tells me this, she creates a web of meaning that would be very difficult to express as a list of steps, but might be represented by a map or flowchart. Writing it down is not her preference. Moreover, a step-by-step text will not adequately convey the interrelationships and the specific knowledge she has about the situation.

Ms. Sullivan puts herself in the situation and writes down a script, much like a performance, of what she might say: "Mr. Brown and Ms. Smith are sick today. When you have finished your area, go clean theirs as well." She offers no specific sequence of directions, but rather believes that her audience will know how to do the work. When I ask her if she can think of more steps, she becomes frustrated and silent. I attempt to help her brainstorm, but she resists. As far as Ms. Sullivan is concerned, the assignment is finished.

At the end of class, Aisha calls on Ms. Collins to read her steps to the class. Ms. Collins is a high school graduate and has solid reading and writing skills. Her response to the question is to call someone who has the day off to come in and work. One step — no problem. Aisha tries to get her to develop the idea more: who will she call, where will they be, what time will she need to call? Ms. Collins looks at Aisha as if she is crazy and explains: "If I was the supervisor, I'd just know it, I wouldn't have to write it down."

The assignment to solve a problem and to write the solution in step-by-step form varies in difficulty for the employees, but few of them produce a sequence of steps because it is not what they usually do and because they do not attach any value to doing so. This is partly because they do not tend to think about the problem sequentially, and partly because they think describing actions with too many words is unnecessary. Thus, they resist being required to do so. The assignment is not simply difficult, it is somehow alien, not a sensible thing to do. As a result, some of the employees, like Ruby, try to think of excuses not to do it. Others, like Mr. Fletcher, try to do what Aisha wants, but cannot. Still others, like Ms. Collins, think the assignment is trivial and give Aisha a hard time verbally instead of doing the writing as required. In each case, there is a subtle layer of resistance to the assignment of writing step-by-step text about something one is called on to do at work.

This tendency to connect self with action rather than with text can also be seen in the writing the employees do in class. One of the women in housekeeping who is asked to write an essay about herself explains: "I don't like to talk too much about myself. You'll have to really spend some time with me and see what I am like and what I like to do." This woman rejects a textual description of herself in favor of developing a relationship, "spend some time together," to develop understanding. Here we are being invited to know her through sharing time and space rather than through exchanging words.

In the conclusion of one of the stories in the Prologue, a housekeeping aide writes: "One day my dream will come true. That's to be a E.K.G. That's my gold." Employees use this type of description frequently. In each case, they use language to connect self to action rather than to separate self from task. What they mean, when I question them further, is that they want to be the person who does the EKG test on patients. But what they tend to say is that they want to be the procedure, not the person who does the procedure.

Workplace Organization

The management at the hospital claims to want and need employees who have better literacy skills, yet the way the workplace is organized for entry-level workers does not require literacy skills to execute job tasks. Much of what employees are required to do is organized around visual rather than verbal sets of instructions. For example, the supplies from the ingredient room in the kitchen are measured, prepackaged, and color coded by a large man who works in the inner sanctum — the ingredient room — so that no reading is required for the preparation of some items. This same method is used in housekeeping. The cleaning supplies are dispensed by a group leader from "the cage," literally a wire structure, and they are often color coded and premixed so that employees have little need to measure or predict amounts. Supervisors often read and write forms and other work-related texts for the employees. What employees are most likely to need to read and write are the grievances and reprimands that are an integral part of the daily life of the hospital. And even more ironic, the process the hospital uses for training new employees reinforces meaning embedded in action rather than description. Mr. Parrott (after Laubach, perhaps) calls it the "each one teach one" method. A new employee is trained by watching an experienced employee clean a room. The new employee is told to watch for mistakes and then go back and correct them. The object for the trainer is to do something that will trick the new employee, such as leaving some dust on a baseboard or forgetting to wipe out a sink. The new employee demonstrates his or her knowledge by correcting the error, by taking action to show that he or she is not fooled. There are training manuals stacked to the ceiling in Mr. Parrott's office, but employees do not use them. Rather, they rely on modeling and apprenticeship forms of teaching.

The Politics of Change

We have seen in this chapter that the ways of constructing and displaying knowledge about work-related tasks are not the same for all program participants. We have also seen that it is often quite difficult for the employees, Aisha, and Karen to recognize the variety of ways in which knowledge is actually made and used at work. As a result, employees are labeled as "in a state of crisis" or "confused." They are described in staff meetings as avoiding the change "inherent in the learning process," as lacking the "humility" to learn. When these interpretations are offered up, Aisha is often silent, unwilling to challenge the descriptions, but convinced they are inaccurate. Moreover, these interpretations are used to justify the need for a curriculum that would formalize their knowledge and make it more consistent — that is, change it into something closer to what mainstream culture recognizes and uses to measure competence.

But as we have seen, employees resist this reformulation. Like Celie, they think that conceiving of job tasks as a series of steps to be written down is something only a fool would do. The next chapter considers the political and social implications work-related text holds for employees, as a way to further understand their resistance to using it in the ways mainstream culture expects.

CHAPTER 5

Reading Texts

To understand more fully employee preference for action over words, for doing something rather than writing about something, it is helpful to examine the ways employees believe text is used at the hospital and what sort of social and political values written words convey to them. One way to start this process of understanding is to examine how employees respond to printed materials in class, at work, and in their lives outside the hospital.

The Curriculum

Based on the literacy audit and interviews with management, Karen and Aisha conclude that curriculum can be based on three areas: the job materials, information about how to transfer to other departments, and information about how to move up within the same department. Although the first area holds promise, curriculum based on how to move up at the hospital proves problematic. There do not seem to be any real incentives to being a team leader, the next step up from entry level. Karen wonders why anyone would want a job that seems to give so little reward for the amount of stress it appears to offer.

Karen's reservations about potential advancement are echoed months later in Ms. Johnson's explanation to Rose about why, after 23 years in an entry-level position, she has no interest in moving ahead:

Rose: Do you ever think about supervising?
Ms. Johnson: I don't think I could stand the stress. You're set up to do a lot of the dirty work. Feedback from everybody. I don't know if I could handle it or not. Ms. Butler has always tried to make me a group leader and stuff like that and I always turn that down.

Ms. Johnson echoes many employees' wish to avoid jobs such as supervisor or group leader. Most of those who want to advance want a new job, out of the kitchen, the laundry, or housekeeping. They want jobs in other areas such as medical records or security.

But in some of these departments, such as security, hiring practices act to eliminate entry-level workers. The security department's tendency to hire only from the outside, for example, leads Karen to decide that perhaps advancement is an unrealistic expectation, and she shifts the focus to generic management or problem-solving skills — things that can help employees with grievances, basic job frustration, and perhaps in personal areas such as parenting skills.

Aisha, however, wants to redefine the issues — to reconceptualize advancement and success based on "what's real" in the lives of the employees and the informal systems operating in the hospital. Essentially, both agendas are incorporated into the lessons, at least at first. The problem-solving scenarios are juxtaposed with Aisha's assignments to learn about the possible. Aisha also quietly adds GED practice activities when she realizes how much employees want them.

By the time Margaret comes to town to evaluate the program after the first few months, three kinds of lessons are being offered in the classes — the job-related curriculum the center has developed, the broader curriculum Aisha has added, and the GED work the employees want. But, as discussed in Chapter 2, Margaret thinks these lessons fail to teach workplace literacy because they look too much like training or general basic skills curriculum rather than a functional context approach.

Margaret blames herself, however, for not doing a good job of teaching Karen and Aisha how to do the literacy audit and the curriculum development. She acknowledges that it is hard, and not everyone has the talent for it. Karen disagrees with her; she thinks they have done a good job in the audit stage but have not gotten it into the lesson plans adequately. Aisha listens quietly, but says very little. Margaret is concerned that what they are developing cannot be used by other employers to develop literacy programs for their own workers. The materials are too local, too particular (and too political) for a demonstration project. She is also concerned that the center might be vulnerable to criticism for not using the funding in the way it has agreed to use it.

Karen listens carefully to Margaret's concerns and then develops a packet of lessons called "Weekly Tips" based on the memoranda sent out by Mr. Parrott to all housekeeping aides. She describes it as combining the functional context approach of using "specific job task content with the principles of scheme and reader response theory." She started working on it before Margaret's arrival, but uses the advice Margaret gives her to "tighten up" the curriculum so it "really looks like the job" and "incorporates the basic skills embedded in the job."

"Weekly Tips" is something Mr. Parrott wants his employees to read and follow, and it is something the employees rarely look at. Supervisors maintain that reading "Weekly Tips" is necessary to do the job well, but the employees see it as unnecessary and time-consuming. For the most part, they believe they know much more than their supervisors do about how to clean and pride themselves on developing procedures that make their work better and more efficient. "If I did it the way he wanted me to, I'd never finish," Ms. Edwards explains.

The packet consists of five weekly tips with themes such as: dust mopping, daily vacuuming, damp mopping of corridors and open areas, damp mopping of patients' rooms, and spray buffing corridors. Preceding each weekly tip sheet in the packet is a series of exercises entitled "Before Reading," including discussion and writing assignments. In a lesson entitled "Before Dust Mopping," for example, the employee is asked to pretend to explain the proper dust mopping techniques to a new employee. Then the employee is told to write the step-by-step directions she would give to the new worker.

After reading the weekly tip on dust mopping, the employee is asked a long series of questions about such information as the heading, the suggested steps for dust mopping, what equipment is used to dust mop, where to change the dusting cloth, and how to store the equipment. Each question assumes the linearity and uniformity of the task, in part because the "Weekly Tips" from which the packet is developed assumes that employees must know how to do a task by conceptualizing it in steps, sequentially, using linguistic clues. But as discussed in Chapter 4, employees generally learn hospital jobs by watching others perform them.

Over the course of the nine months, however, sequencing tasks and describing them with language, either orally or in written text, are the main themes of the curriculum. As the employees become more used to these lessons, they develop the ability to perform the tasks the way Margaret and Karen expect them to. But they tend to think of the sequencing as redundant and boring. "Not this again," they whisper to me when the lessons are introduced.

Amanda has a similar experience with the supervisors' class. These employees hold more prestigious positions than the entry-level employees, and they need literacy skills to do their work. They often write up reports, grievances, and reprimands. They keep track of the time sheets and fill out other paperwork for their employees, such as passes to the clinic. These women, however, also tend to think in holistic terms. Amanda analyzes it this way in her journal:

> Neither student could look at her job in discrete segments. Neither could describe what she did. When asked to describe the job, she said it took patience and hard work to do. Each generalized about the job in terms of the tasks.

What is interesting in this passage is that women who are working on the supervisory level, using text every day, still appear to Amanda not to be sequential thinkers. They still tend to think in more general or holistic ways about their tasks and to map meaning onto action rather than onto text or words. What Amanda observes in the supervisors' class and what I observe in the entry-level workers' classes confirm that it is possible to be literate and to think in ways that are connected and holistic rather than step by step. It is possible to be literate and not be the "new person" many workplace literacy programs aim to produce. It is also possible, of course, to be literate and incompetent at the same time.

Resistance to Job Texts

The "Weekly Tips" packet takes Karen a long time to produce and has a variety of activities for employees to perform. It is designed to be used for one whole six-week session at the beginning of the summer. When Aisha first takes the packet to class and starts to use it, employees cooperate and do the assignments. Some work quickly and do very well; others work more slowly. Aisha assigns some of the lessons for homework. Karen believes she has developed the closest thing yet to what Margaret wants. The employees hate it. But they don't say so — at least not at first.

There are three ways that employees tend to respond to the lessons. A group of them simply stop coming to class. Another group tries to finish the work as quickly as possible. Ms. Rivers, who sometimes works the night shift in the nursery after a day shift in housekeeping, finishes the packet at three o'clock one morning between changing diapers and soothing crying infants. Other employees respond to the assignments with a subtle form of resistance. They say they've lost the packet. Someone has borrowed it, but they can't remember who. Or they left it in the car, and it's too hot to go get it. Or they have finished it already, but have left it at home. Others struggle patiently.

Mr. Stone tends to take the exercises and change them into something he is interested in. He does this all along, even before "Weekly Tips" is introduced. One day in class, Aisha assigns an essay based on a set of words drawn from work. Instead of writing about work using the words, Mr. Stone chooses to write about things of importance to him — his son and his free time.

VACATION BREAK

My son and I went on a holiday *vacation*. Although we didn't have no *schedule* and most of the time no *break* simple because we didn't want to loose any time. And we *shift* drivers to take over and rest while one drive and the other rest. *Authority* was in both our hand because we are the driver and we check the *calendar* and we really didn't have much time. On the vacation break but we really had a good time. And no *overtime* was in our plan but we needed each other love and father and son, and we was both the *supervisor*.

When Mr. Stone writes this essay, he is hoping to drive to Chicago to get his son on Labor Day. He ends up having to work instead. Mr. Stone refuses to stay hooked to the job task even when the assignment demands it. Given a vocabulary exercise using words from work, he is able to fashion a story that resonates with his own life experience, something that matters to him. Mr. Stone needs for his text to be personally meaningful, and he makes it so despite the assignment.

Aisha also resists or changes many of the assignments. She uses her oft-repeated condemnation, "dry as dust" — the same description Karen uses about the job texts in general — to describe the assignments to Amanda and me. Aisha does try to focus her lessons on the job-related curriculum for at least part of each class. However, she generally leaves some time in class for other activities. "We need to give them the gift of something they want," she explains. As her own form of resistance she brings in other things to read and discuss, such as copies of Shay Youngblood's "Snuff Dippers," a short story about upper-class White-folks who are run over by a truck after tormenting several Black house-keepers riding the bus home from work. Ms. Edwards and I take turns reading it out loud to each other, and when we finish, she tells me it is one of the best things she has ever read.

Another time, Mr. Stone brings in an article from *Jet* about a five hundred pound lady who sat on her husband and killed him. Aisha laughs and tells him, "I was hoping no one would see it [the article]," but she is not serious. She spends a great deal of time in class talking about and letting employees read the story, and then she explains to me (because I am the only White person in the class) that "When something like this happens, Black people just pray that somebody White did it."

This launches a discussion about how terribly embarrassed the community is when a bizarre crime turns out to be committed by one of their own, which gives me an insight into how vulnerable some of these men and women feel. Their remarks reveal a sense of exposure and a genuine concern for appearances. Aisha uses the opportunity provided by Mr. Stone's article to initiate a discussion about community pride and identity. It has nothing to do with the skills that are embedded in the job tasks, but it has everything to do with why the employees have come to class in the first place. In encouraging this class discussion, Aisha resists staying hooked into the job tasks and pursues her own goals of developing self-esteem and a critical consciousness.

When the "Weekly Tips" assignment draws to a close, the remaining employees are especially pleased. Aisha is out of class one day and Rose takes her place. Someone asks if they are going to do "Weekly Tips" today and Rose tells her no. Ms. Benson shouts, "Thank you," and Ms. Edwards exclaims, "So we off that 'Weekly Tips' junk? I don't want to know nothing about no mopping and no dusting." The others laugh. Later, when Rose tries to collect each employee's completed packet, Ms. Redding looks at her with a masterfully deadpan expression and innocently explains, "Me and 'Weekly Tips' done fell out. I threw mines away. Mr. Fletcher, too. We did it together." Later, she grins at me and slips it out of her notebook, where she has hidden it for the last few weeks, and hands it in. She says she is just "talkin' junk." But she makes it clear that she doesn't like the assignment and asks that we not have any others like it.

At the next class meeting, Aisha asks Ms. Redding what she likes best in class. Ms. Redding replies that her favorite assignment for the whole time she has come to class is the essay she wrote six months earlier on *Raisin in the Sun*. She hands that in, too, and asks Aisha to keep it in her file. This is the lesson that Margaret has described as "shoddy," the least hooked to the job tasks. There is more than a little irony in the remark. Although Margaret is concerned about lessons that develop metacognitive skills and fulfill the intent of the grant, Ms. Redding finds these lessons boring and insulting, not worth her time. Instead, she values the assignment to watch a movie and to write a personal response to what she believes to be a meaningful story.

When Ms. Johnson is interviewed at the end of the project, she says she thinks "Weekly Tips" is "for the pits." She continues:

I've been at King Memorial for 23 years, and I feel like if I don't
know how to clean now, I will not learn. . . . That's not going to
help me get my GED I don't think. I don't think it will.

When Ms. Morrison is asked what she would change about the classes
she says:

That part about mopping. To me it was boring cause everybody
know how to mop. I liked current events and everything very
much, but when it comes to mopping, mmm-mm. The things you
do every day? Just like little kids, they get bored. Have this big ole
book? Just about the whole thing about mopping.

When Rose asks her a related question she criticizes the writing assignments related to the job tasks: "I didn't like rewriting things concerning
mopping, cleaning, and dish washing. I felt I already knowed that."
Other women tell Amanda that they have dropped out of class because
they think "Weekly Tips" is insulting.

Text and Social Organization

Although employees do not like "Weekly Tips," it would be simplistic to assume that content alone is the problem. The lack of employee
interest in the lessons is further complicated by a failure to consider that
for these workers, job texts cannot be easily separated from their political and social purposes. In order to see this, we must look at the broader
ways in which King employees tend to value and use text at work. For
example, two features of "Weekly Tips" doom it to failure before it is
even considered to generate curriculum.

First, "Weekly Tips" is written by Mr. Parrott. As discussed in Chapter 3, he is extremely unpopular with many of his employees. They
consider him arrogant, insensitive, and unfair. They talk about his sexual exploits, his drunk-driving record, and his misogyny. Furthermore,
they do not think he knows nearly as much as they do about how to do
their jobs. For these employees, text is the embodiment of the person
who writes it. They do not automatically separate the text from the
writer, the doer from the deed. So, they think of Mr. Parrott when they
read his memoranda. They do not look at "Weekly Tips" as just a piece
of text. Reading these memoranda and doing the exercises in the packets
are like being right in the room with Mr. Parrott.

This connection of text to the context of its production makes
"Weekly Tips" something to be avoided even though a good number of

employees are able to read it. They often resist following Mr. Parrott's instructions as a matter of choice, not because they lack the basic skills to do so. Some employees do lack the skills, but many others do not. In either case, "Weekly Tips" is something to avoid or ignore rather than something to read.

The second reason "Weekly Tips" is so unpopular is that text at the hospital does not always reflect employees' lived experience. Employees do not trust it, and do not think it descriptive of what actually goes on. Aisha encourages this kind of critical thinking in class. She is constantly asking the employees to tell her the story behind the story, comparing what the text says to do with what employees in fact do. Evaluation of text is an ongoing issue in the weekly staff meetings:

> *Karen:* It doesn't matter if "Weekly Tips" is real or not. They need to be able to read it. Those supervisors think its real.
> *Aisha:* It's posted, its everywhere, but they don't read it. It's our expectations bumped up against what's really there.

In a later meeting, when the lesson includes the steps to follow when the incinerator used to burn the toxic waste is not working, Aisha brings this issue up again:

> *Aisha:* The waste thing. Clarence and Mr. Fletcher can tell you the real issues surrounding how they have to dispose of that very dangerous stuff. They told me it didn't really work the way it was written down, so I told them to write down what really exists. Clarence wants to write a letter with the whole class to protest.
> *Sarah:* It gets funny with questions like this when from experience they know that all you have to do to fix the incinerator is go around and kick it. And we don't want to give the impression that somehow literacy is tied up with ignoring common sense and not using your head and that could be an interesting . . .
> *Rose:* But we're not, we're saying according to the steps listed in the paper, according to the text.
> *Sarah:* Right, right, that's an interesting thing talking about emphasizing that's not necessarily the way you really do it.
> *Aisha:* What do you bring that you already know.
> *Karen:* Oh, yeah, sometimes texts really aren't reality. But that doesn't mean you can't be able to read it.

Karen and Rose are beginning to acknowledge that texts and experience are often different at the hospital, but they still believe that employees ought to be able to read them. However, they cannot account for the fact that employees consciously choose not to read texts because they believe the texts are wrong, or because not reading them or acting as if they do not read them is an act of resistance.

Aisha and Sarah, on the other hand, are more concerned with the underlying political issues inherent in this situation. They are suspicious, at least, that the issue of text dependency is more complex than it first appears. Early in the project Aisha suspects that employees are engaged in resistance, but she does not voice these concerns until the final month of the project.

Ways with Text

King employees make contact with several types of text at the hospital. The entry-level employees are most often the recipients of this text rather than its producers. It is distributed to them in a variety of ways. Certain kinds of text are posted throughout the hospital. Other pieces of text are enclosed in employee pay envelopes. Finally, notebooks, bound booklets, and other packets have been collected in certain places, such as Mr. Parrott's office, so that employees can refer to them for information. Most of this text is generated by management and the personnel office.

Text to Describe

A large proportion of this text is descriptive in nature. Examples include notices about spaces in the new parking deck, flyers for an upcoming training class, or the biweekly hospital newsletter. This text is written in a simple, clear, and concise manner. Its goal is to disseminate information to the hospital community. All employees receive these descriptive texts.

Text to Define

Other pieces of text contain procedural information. These texts are normative rather than descriptive. That is, they focus on what employees should or must do. "Weekly Tips" is an example of text that defines behavior. In the hospital there are volumes of text written about rules and regulations. Employees are expected to follow these written-down rules, and when they do not, they risk being labeled illiterate. However, as I spend time in the hospital and talk with the employees I realize that written-down procedures are not followed even by those who can read them. One day in class, the disparity between texts and experience, and the hostility and frustration of those who are powerless to control the production and use of text, becomes especially focused.

One of the most important documents in the hospital for employees to read lists the universal precautions for dealing with potentially dangerous substances such as needles and other paraphernalia used in the care of AIDS patients. A lesson is developed from procedures for emptying the Sharpes needle container. This is one of the jobs of Ms. Edwards, who cleans an area of the hospital where there are several AIDS patients.

Aisha asks her to explain the universal precautions for emptying the Sharpes container. The question is fairly straightforward, but in her response, Ms. Edwards opens a window of understanding, a glimpse of the political nature of texts in the hospital:

> *Ms. Edwards:* There's the danger that one of the needles that sticking out may come out. And sometimes the nurses they'll have the needle container too full.
>
> *Mr. Stone:* All the time.
>
> *Ms. Edwards:* All the time, you right. Well, sometime on my area cause I try to check mines every day because I'm the one handling them. Because, like I was telling my supervisor, some of them is real careless. They don't care cause they don't have to take that thing up and down, see and I been stuck three times since I been working over there.

Aisha tries to focus the class away from Ms. Edwards's analysis of the situation, her dependence on the local knowledge of emptying the containers, and toward the content of the text, the actual written-down sequence the supervisors claim Ms. Edwards does not follow because she cannot read very well.

Aisha continues to read the handout, which says to do everything while the container is still on the wall. But Ms. Edwards explains that she always takes it off the wall first to line everything up because sometimes the container is too full. By this point in the class the employees are used to step-by-step assignments, so Aisha, Ms. Edwards, and Mr. Stone reorganize the steps according to the information Ms. Edwards has shared. They compare taking down and putting up. Mr. Stone then begins to critique the text. He reminds the class that the first step is always "put on your gloves" even though the text (universal precautions) does not state it. Ms. Edwards is, however, still not satisfied with the steps Aisha has helped them develop. She repeats again her procedure of taking the container off the wall before she puts the cover on:

> *Ms. Edwards:* Well, I take it off the wall and put it on the floor and shake it down because a lot of them needles don't be down in there, they be sticking out the top . . .
>
> *Mr. Stone:* Sticking all *out* the top. They [doctors and nurses] don't care. They just [makes a motion like flicking away flies while hissing disgust through his teeth].
>
> *Ms. Edwards:* Well, see, they don't have to move them.
>
> *Aisha:* How far up do the needles go in the box and how do I know how full to make the box? Is there a line?
>
> *Ms. Edwards:* To that line [pointing to the line on the box].
>
> *Aisha:* Where's the line? [Aisha can't see the line because she is behind the box and behind the desk.]
>
> *Mr. Stone:* Turn it all around to the front. Read the white sticker on the front.
>
> *Aisha (reading the sticker):* Do not fill above this level.
>
> *Mr. Stone:* Thank you.
>
> *Aisha:* So, I'm in trouble if this is off of the box, aren't I?
>
> *Mr. Stone:* They don't care nothing about that.
>
> *Aisha:* Yeah, I know that.
>
> *Ms. Edwards:* If that seal is off of the box, um, you will be in trouble in one way.
>
> *Aisha:* Um-hum, how?
>
> *Ms. Edwards:* Um, most peoples wouldn't look at how far to fill it. Some of them, uh, don't pay attention.
>
> *Mr. Stone:* Naw, they don't care.
>
> *Aisha:* They really don't look at that line?
>
> *Ms. Edwards:* They won't look at that line most of the time. They have 'em sticking all out the box.
>
> *Mr. Stone:* RNs, LPNs . . .
>
> *Aisha (laughing):* You want to get them labeled, don't you? RNs, LPNs — and MDs?
>
> *Mr. Stone:* That's right.
>
> *Ms. Edwards:* That's the reason why, when I unlock it, I sit the whole container on the floor . . . and I shake it and level them down cause you go to put that seal on and some of them needles be sticking straight out.
>
> *Aisha:* Put it on a level surface.
>
> *Ms. Edwards:* Um-hum, and make sure that there's not any sticking out those little cracks in the side.

Aisha: There's another reason of making sure it's snapped.

Ms. Edwards: But I have . . .

Aisha: Cause they can't if it's snapped tightly.

Mr. Stone: They really don't do it right. The nurses don't. They stick the needle like this [he uses his hands to show putting the needle in the container with the business end sticking up rather than down]. They not supposed to do that. You supposed to break the top off the needles and drop the needles in.

Ms. Edwards: But they don't do it. Them needles, them sharp, them uh, heads be sticking all out the top of that . . .

Aisha: I've seen them do that where they do the procedure and put it right on your food tray. You go to pick it up and you could get stuck.

Mr. Stone: That's right.

Ms. Edwards: Well, I have found them on the sink, you know, when you go to wash the sink in the hospital?

Mr. Stone: Yes, indeed.

Ms. Edwards: Needle be laying up there and one day, I got stuck with one like that. Laying up on the sink, somebody left it there. They be on the floor on my area all the time. You tell the head nurse and it don't do any good. The next day, you go back. You find another one. I leave 'em there, I don't touch 'em. I leave 'em right down on the floor. Mop all around 'em.

At this point in the class, there is a heavy silence as the enormity of her words seeps in. What emerges from this discussion is a picture of literate and powerful doctors and nurses not following the content of the text. The result of this ignoring of text, or lack of text dependency, is possible injury not to themselves but to those employees, like Ms. Edwards and Mr. Stone, who have the least control over the enforcement of policy. Text becomes not just simply something one does not or cannot read, it becomes a false reality that literate employees also ignore. Dependency on text is not exhibited by those with power and authority in the hospital, so the employees see themselves as having to deal with their lived experience instead of what it says on paper. But most of the employees who work with used needles seem to know correct handling procedures, even though those with more power do not follow them.

But there is a further irony here. As discussed in Chapter 3, the state legislature recently made King Memorial exempt from liability. Even if Ms. Edwards were to contract AIDS due to another employee's negligence, there is a text that says the hospital would bear no legal

responsibility for her condition. In this case, attempting to make employees text dependent raises ethical issues of authority and control that
help explain why some employees are so resistant to basing their knowledge on what is written in a book. They believe that only a person with
no common sense, a person who is docile and easily manipulated, would
accept everything that is written down.

I experience a somewhat similar situation as a volunteer in the
hospital. When I am in training, I receive a list of universal precautions
to protect myself and those patients I care for against infection. The
procedures include elaborate hand-washing and gown-changing rituals
between caring for each patient. However, when I actually begin to
work on the floor, I realize that no one follows the procedures, and I am
told by more than one nurse that I do not have to either as long as I
follow them when certain people are there observing. Again, the text I
am told to follow is a false reality for the work I actually do.

Text to Control

In other instances, employees see text not as a false reality but as a
means of control. The ability to use text or not use it in the manner
deemed necessary becomes the very means of establishing the borders of
control over employees. Of all the official text in the hospital, "Standards of Conduct" in the employee handbook is the most controlling
and negative in tone. It actually delineates a formal set of consequences
for inappropriate behavior on the job. There is no setting out of the
standards employees are expected to uphold in this section, merely a
detailed list of what happens when they do not follow the rules. The
employee must infer from the text what positive behaviors are expected.
In addition, terms such as "progressive discipline" and "rehabilitation"
carry normative messages expressed in negative terms. In order to give
the document more authority and to make it more inaccessible to its
readers, the language is convoluted and obscure. In the supervisors'
class, Amanda uses "Standards of Conduct" as a text to understand and
rewrite in more accessible, less threatening language. Here is her description of what happens:

> The students said working with the "Standards of Conduct" was
> the most valuable part of the course. They have to use "Standards
> of Conduct" with their employees and hadn't known what it
> meant. They used the words, but didn't know meaning. They, pre-
> viously, felt very frustrated by it. There were several sentences they
> never did understand. They wrote several revisions of the stan-

dards; however, in essence, they wrote what they thought needed to be included, without deciphering the document.

"Standards of Conduct" is not the only text used to control behavior; supervisors use other forms of text to maintain their power. Mr. Stone discovers this when he has a disagreement with Ms. Butler. Instead of accepting what she says, he disagrees with her openly. The consequences of his resistance to her authority are mediated by text:

> *Mr. Stone:* She just, y'know, doing like she want to do. Then like when our evaluation comes up an' she sits down and dos the evaluation and all we have to do is sign it, and tell her, "This ain't right," she go, "You gonna sign it." And she forged my name on a reprimand.
>
> *Gowen:* She forged your name on a reprimand?
>
> *Mr. Stone:* Forged, forged my name, sure did. That's why I didn't get my job. When I went up for this other job, in the maintenance shop? She had done forged my name, put it in my file. A reprimand, that's why I didn't get that job. Cause I sure had the job, already told. Talked to the dude. He told me I could get it. And then he told me, "There's a reprimand in your file." "There's a reprimand in my file?" He said, "Yeah, sure is."
>
> *Gowen:* Is there anything you can do about that?
>
> *Mr. Stone:* Not now, if I do something it gotta be like five days from when I first find out. See, I didn't know about it. I thought she, I didn't know it was even in there. I didn't sign it, I told her, "That ain't right." I say, "Nothing on this thing is right and you know it." She say, "I know how to run my job, you don't know how to do yours. You don't do this and you don't do that." I do what I'm supposed to do. I supposed to do two floors, I supposed to do four and two. And I do most of them and every time I look around, it don't never satisfy her. If you don't, if you don't run it behind her, you know, so to speak . . .
>
> *Gowen:* What does that mean, run it behind her?
>
> *Mr. Stone:* Do like she, do what she wants, you know.

Mr. Stone sees his supervisor as someone who uses texts to tell lies and to punish him and to do it in a manner that makes it beyond question. He essentially feels powerless when Ms. Butler writes reprimands for his file. He sees texts at work as representing the authority that holds him down, that calls him stupid, that keeps him out.

He also feels marginalized because he does not have the credentials to certify that he can use text. He tells me that because he has not finished high school, Ms. Butler assumes he does not know anything:

> She have picks, certain people she do certain things for. She don't think I'm smart enough to know that, but I told her just because I didn't go all the way through school, don't mean I'm no fool. I know what be going on. She told me I notice too much. It's not the idea that I notice too much, if my eyes see it I can't help but notice it.

In this case, Mr. Stone is categorized in a certain way because he had no certificate, no "piece of paper," no text to define him as knowledgeable. He resents this category and the powerlessness it bestows on its members. As Ms. Edwards tells me one day, "If you don't have that piece of paper they do you any kinda way."

In addition to writing reprimands and grievances, supervisors also use memoranda to exert control. Here is an example of a memorandum Ms. Edwards receives from her supervisor. Notice how the text is not error free. I point this out to Ms. Edwards when she shows it to me, and she is stunned that someone who has earned the GED and been promoted to supervisor is still not writing perfect standard English. She does not think that is possible.

Memo To: Ms. Carolyn Edwards

From: Ms. LaShaundra Harris

Re: Changing of Schedule

This memo is to formerly address the change in your schedule. Due to the way the areas are designated it is very important that I change your schedule to better accommodate the hospital. Your services will be needed and are much needed to cover the patient area on weekends. Effective July 10 your schedule will change to a rotating weekends. The hospital can no longer draft overtime to cover area in which we have personnel who can work. Most area cleaners work weekends unless their areas of responsibility is closed. Ms. Edwards you are responsible for servicing 14a Backhall and Nurses station these areas are not closed and does need servicing on weekends.

Ms. Harris uses this memorandum to tell Ms. Edwards her schedule has been changed. But there is a long story behind this text that suggests its purpose is more than informational. This story is alluded to briefly in Chapter 3. What follows is a more complete version.

Ms. Edwards has been working at King Memorial for six years as a housekeeping aide. When she took the position, it was a five-day-a-week job, leaving the weekends for Ms. Edwards to spend with her family, care for her bedridden mother-in-law, and go to church on Sundays. Everything goes just fine on her job until a few months after the literacy classes start. She is rarely absent from class and receives good evaluations from her supervisor, whom she likes very much.

When the literacy classes begin, her supervisor encourages her to enroll. Ms. Edwards does so because she has always wanted to complete her education and get her GED. Ultimately she wants to move up, but she knows she cannot without "that piece of paper." She is very energetic and enthusiastic when she comes to class, although Rose realizes quickly that reading and writing are difficult for Ms. Edwards. But she is eager and learns very quickly. Her high spirits lift everyone up and she is a valuable addition to the class. Aisha especially likes her "because she is so feisty."

After a few months of class, Ms. Edwards's supervisor is transferred and a new woman takes her place. Actually, the new supervisor originally held Ms. Edwards's current job, but has taken a leave of absence, earned her GED, and returned in a higher position. It is at this point that things become complicated. Ms. Edwards finds the new supervisor, Ms. Harris, abrasive and demanding.

Ms. Harris is younger than Ms. Edwards, and she seems to try to make Ms. Edwards's life miserable. She starts out by doing "finger checks" on the walls in the rooms Ms. Edwards is assigned to clean, looking for dust. This makes Ms. Edwards angry, and she informs Ms. Harris that no one ever did that when Ms. Harris had the job, and that she does the job better than Ms. Harris ever did anyway.

After a few days, Ms. Harris starts finding work for Ms. Edwards to do right at the time she is supposed to be coming to class. This irritates Ms. Edwards so much that she goes to the assistant manager and complains. At this point, Ms. Harris tells Ms. Edwards that from now on, she will have to work every other weekend. Ms. Edwards then demands an interview with the assistant manager over the matter. This puts the issue out on the table, and Ms. Edwards explains her position to the assistant manager. It is at this point that they have the meeting referred to in Chapter 3.

After the meeting, Ms. Harris writes Ms. Edwards the memorandum above. After Ms. Edwards receives the memorandum, she knows she has to submit and give up every other weekend with her family. She is both angry and hurt.

Text Outside of Work

To characterize employees as "not text-dependent people" is to assume that they respond to all text in the same way. It is also to assume that the specific nature of a piece of text does not affect a person's response to and valuation of it. This, however, is not the case with the learners in the literacy classes.

For example, Mr. Stone does not perceive all text in a negative manner. There are two formalized texts that Mr. Stone values deeply. First is his GED preparation book. It is a monstrous tome, and he has worked through many of the exercises on his own. He has had the book since he took the GED classes a few years ago. During the project I occasionally help him with lessons in the book. He fights with it, but he is determined to master its content. It symbolizes the key to a new future — a transformation — a life of security rather than struggle, of dignity rather than denial.

The Bible is Mr. Stone's other prized text. He is a member of the Temple of Holy Prayer. When my family and I attend church with Mr. Stone, we are able to see him in a different setting. Here, in the cool sanctuary, we sit with Mr. Stone through five hours of Sunday school and church. During this time, Mr. Stone follows the lessons and the oral readings in his Bible — a large book that he keeps protected in a rich brown leather zippered case. Inside he carries a yellow highlighter and several pens and pencils. His book is well marked. The services we attend focus on the words in the Bible. The minister spends most of his time reading the words and then explaining what they mean. Mr. Stone follows and highlights the words as the minister reads the text. Then, as the minister talks about the text, Mr. Stone makes notes in the margins and underlines important passages again in pen.

In addition to attending five hours of church every Sunday when he has the day off, Mr. Stone also attends Bible study on Wednesday evenings. During these lessons he spends more time hearing, reading, and interpreting text. If asked, he can quote a vast amount of biblical text verbatim and then explain what the text means to him and how he might apply it in everyday experiences. For example, Mr. Stone is very aware of the power of separation. He maintains that Ms. Butler uses techniques of separation to undermine the men and women who work under her:

> I told her [Ms. Butler] she was just like the Pharaoh, in the Bible.
> Kept the slaves fighting among themselves. Keeping them a fight-
> ing so they won't think.

Mr. Stone observes that the Pharaoh was smart to keep all the slaves
divided and fighting among themselves. He explains that it kept them
from realizing the conditions of their slavery. The same tactic serves to
maintain the power relationships Ms. Butler relies on to control her
employees.

In observing Mr. Stone in settings outside of work, I come to believe
that the texts Mr. Stone resists reading and using in his daily work are
the texts of the job that are punitive and that categorize him as incompetent. Other texts, however, are very important to him. Magazines
such as *Jet* and the newspaper are among the texts he values and wishes
to know more about. They are texts that are not incorporated into the
functional context curriculum because they do not "hook right back into
the job tasks."

This differentiation between texts to read and texts to ignore is true
for other employees as well. Ms. Collins, who says she and "'Weekly
Tips' done fell out" is an avid reader. She tells Rose in an interview: "I
read the paper, magazines. I used to read novels, too. I read the paper
from one end to the other." She often mentions some article she has read
in the paper in class. Ms. Sullivan and Mr. Fletcher read novels, including Mr. Fletcher's favorite, *Great Expectations*. When Rose asks Ms.
Sullivan if she reads more now that she is coming to the literacy classes,
Ms. Sullivan responds: "Well, before I have attended the class I have
always read. I love reading anyway."

Ms. Edwards prefers to read her church bulletin, recipes, and mail-
order catalogues. One day she brings Rose a recipe for buttermilk pie.
Another day she brings a mail-order catalogue to class to show me a
closet organizer for storing purses that she wants to order. She has so
many purses she cannot keep up with them, and she wants to arrange
them more carefully in one of the three closets she uses to store her
clothes. Another day we talk about a meat loaf recipe and, knowing
how text dependent I am, Ms. Edwards tells me to be sure and make my
grocery list before I go to the store so I won't forget any of the ingredients: "Make sure and write it down 'cause you might forget." Then she
laughs at her own joke.

Ms. Johnson has her grandchildren write letters to her son (their
father) whenever they come to her house for a visit. Her son has
divorced their mother and has remarried. He serves in the Air Force and
is stationed in Germany. Ms. Johnson believes it is important for her

grandchildren to write letters to their father, so she supervises the activity when she can. She also writes letters to her son, although she prefers using the telephone to communicate with other family members. Most of Ms. Johnson's writing is bill paying, but she believes she is a good writer, and says she enjoys writing.

Some of the hospital employees run a numbers operation to supplement their incomes. They are very careful with their record keeping, using text daily to record bets and tabulate payoffs. These employees value and respect the power of text and literacy, but not for learning how to dust or mop. Rather, their uses of text focus on developing and sustaining a self-owned business to supplement their meager incomes. Other employees also have businesses on the side. The same men and women who are characterized as "confused" or "unorganized" run catering services, repair cars and small appliances, provide child care for pay, direct youth programs at their churches, and organize their communities to provide services for the homeless.

Text and Power

In examining the kinds of text employees most often encounter at work, one can draw several conclusions. First, text is used to reproduce the organizational system of the hospital. The text is used to give information, to set forth rules and regulations, and to punish or reprimand. Second, in very few cases is text used toward more positive ends. None of the employees I interview, for example, can remember ever receiving a memorandum complimenting them on their work. Amanda also observes this in her notes:

> The idea of giving positive feedback was new to them. Neither student had ever done that and didn't know how. They tried giving compliments and found it successful. I doubt they continued it. It was too new of an idea *and there was no reinforcement to do it.* (emphasis added)

Not surprisingly, none of the employees I interview express any pleasure or fondness for the texts of the institution. Their beliefs about the hospital texts are either neutral or negative. This is partly because the knowledge such texts reproduce is often considered inaccurate, particularly when the text describes job performance. It is also partly because the text is written in language that is both inaccessible and harsh. As Amanda notes, many employees read it, but do not understand what they are reading.

Finally, other text, such as notices about benefits and payroll, are considered important by some but not all of the employees. Many employees, like Geraldine, read everything and are well versed in hospital policy. Others, such as Ms. Harold, tend not to look at text, even the notices that are sent to her in her pay envelope. But to conclude that Ms. Harold does not read text because she cannot read is inaccurate. Rather, she and many other employees often make active choices not to read the hospital text, relying instead on the informal networks of oral communication to acquire and display the knowledge they need to work at King Memorial.

The next chapter describes what the employees want from a literacy program at work and how Aisha tries to give them at least a part of what they want. The value-neutral model of teaching the job skills embedded in tasks and reading workplace texts is not broad enough to account for the social and political dimensions of the texts and their potential to be used not for enlightenment but for oppression or abuse.

CHAPTER 6

Listening to Workers

When the center begins to develop its literacy program, it hopes to attract most of the over 100 employees working in entry-level jobs at the hospital. And sixty-five employees do attend at least one of the classes, but only 20 come consistently over the nine months of the project. It is difficult to speculate on why so few employees take advantage of the classes. It is more revealing to consider what motivates those who do come to class. This chapter discusses these motivating factors and also considers how they differ from the reasons management wants its employees to improve their literacy skills.

The differences between employer and employee goals are not readily apparent when the project begins. They surface during the initial literacy task analysis, and become much more pronounced over the course of the project. Most employees come to learn new skills. But few of them see themselves as confused, unorganized, or incompetent—definitions provided by management. Rather, they come to class for their own reasons. They resist the program's narrow categories and attempt to learn what they believe they need to reach their own personal goals. As Ms. Edwards explains: "Sometimes you have to take what you get and make the best of it." In the initial data forms, employees are asked to list why they are attending class (see Table 6.1). The information from these forms indicates that employees' goals are quite different from those of their employer, and they become more at ease in the classes, they begin to discuss their goals more openly.

EMPLOYEES' GOALS: "Gettin' out"

As Margaret predicts, some of the employees say they want to move up. They come to class hoping they will learn what they need to advance in the hospital. How that translates for them is, however, quite different from how it translates for those who plan the program. They

Table 6.1. Reasons for Attending Work Skills
            Development Classes

Reason	Number
"Getting out"	
Getting a better job/more money	22
Getting more education (including a GED)	17
Learning specific skills	3
Improving current job performance	2
	44
"Making myself whole"	
Self-improvement (in general)	12
Getting more education (including a GED)	17
Improving oral communication skills	5
Helping family members	12
	46

often speak of escape, of "gettin' out" of their present jobs. Their words reflect a feeling of being trapped in jobs they do not find rewarding. Some have a certain job in mind; others simply want to "advance themselves." They want out of the enclosed jobs that many of them, especially the women, have had for most of their adult lives.

First of all, there are the employees who are interested in specific jobs. These men and women want the particular training, the distinct skills required to perform the job. Unwilling and unlikely to look at the global nature of job skills in the way the literacy providers expect them to, they want the specific, idiographic knowledge for a particular occupation. If they are, for example, interested in moving into security, they want to learn the actual skills required for this specific job. They are not always able to articulate what these skills are exactly, but they have some idea of what they are not. They believe that reading "Weekly Tips," for example, will do little to win them a job in the security department.

Few of them see how learning a set of metacognitive skills embedded in their present jobs is necessary or sufficient for job advancement. As discussed in Chapter 4, none of them think of skills as universally embedded in a variety of different tasks. What they are expecting to learn and what they are expected to learn are two (or more) different things. This results in disappointment for some of the employees who come to the first six-week session. Many of them drop out because they do not believe they need literacy skills, which is what the classes are actually teaching, no matter what euphemism is chosen as the title. These employees want more and decide to find other ways to get it.

Margaret and Karen assume that all jobs require some of the same skills; employees view each particular job as requiring a unique repertoire of skills. This is a major difference in the way the two groups process their experiences. Time and again the curriculum includes a lesson about some hospital procedure that is supposed to be representative of any one of a number of procedures. For example, one day the lesson consists of reading a pay stub and determining whether the employee has been paid correctly. Ms. Edwards describes the process in her department and then says she does not know how it is done in other places. Aisha tells her that it is the same in all departments because it is more efficient for the hospital to do it this way. But this one explanation is not enough. Time and again, during the entire nine months of instruction, the words, "I don't know how you all do it, but in our department we do it this way," are used to answer a question about general hospital procedures.

Employees simply do not think that things are done the same way everywhere. Furthermore, working at King Memorial tends to confirm this belief. Although the hospital has certain policies that are supposed to apply across the board, they are executed differently by different supervisors. The employees sense that they need to know the specific representation of the event in their own lives much more than they need to know the general rule. In a sense, the resistance to decontextualizing knowledge, to generalizing rules and procedures, is an effort to maintain a competence of the particular, a knowledge of their own personal situations. Ultimately this might be described as a kind of literacy that requires reading the text of one's own life experience, one's own possibilities and constraints in order to learn the knowledge and skills needed to survive.

As a result, many employees say they want better jobs, and they know the official procedures, but they believe a hidden agenda prevents them from advancing. Recall again the point Brenda makes at the end of the first session of classes (Chapter 2):

> I get depressed because I don't make no money. It adds burdens. I got big ideas, that's my problem. That's the way I think. I don't feel like I belong where I am. . . . The problem is you get branded in a certain role and they won't let you get no other jobs. . . . We don't get the cooperation you do from the supervisors. They're not interested in us. We haven't gotten a raise in five years.

Brenda expresses a common belief: Someone or something is keeping them out of the jobs they want. They are stuck on the bottom. No matter how much they want out, no matter how hard they try, they are always held back, overlooked, left behind. The promise of classes that will teach them new skills is the first hope many employees have felt in years. When they discover that the classes are actually literacy classes instead of specific job skills training, some of them are bitterly disappointed.

This view of entry-level employees as stuck on the bottom is also held by at least some managers and supervisors. When Margaret, Karen, and Aisha first meet with Mr. Parrott, he is scornful of trying to teach literacy skills to increase employees' chances of being promoted. He wants to know what is in it for his workers, and when Margaret suggests promotions, he explains that his people are never promoted even when they are well qualified for a job. He is candid and a little hostile, but not rude. He explains that his employees are on the bottom and he believes they are doomed to stay there — with or without a literacy program. For Mr. Parrott, the suggestion of advancement for housekeeping aides is unrealistic and unfair.

Many employees are able to name specific jobs they want to try for, such as being an area clerk or working in medical records. These are exactly the jobs management suggests they can move into with adequate literacy skills. Others, however, talk of wanting a better job, transferring to another department, or making more money in less specific terms. They want something better, but they are not quite sure what. As part of the assessment of the project, Rose asks employees what their job objectives are, and if they have been met.

Rose: Did you want to move up at King?
Ms. Johnson: I couldn't decide what I want to do, you know?

Rose: Do you have any plans for moving up?
Ms. Robbins: I do want to. I want a data entry position, but I know that I will have to take some night courses or something.
Rose: They teach a class here [at the hospital] in typing.
Ms. Robbins: I didn't know that.

Mr. Stone tells me he wants to work in security, but he has no idea what he needs to do to apply for the position. Another woman also tells me she wants a job in security: "I have applied for it several times, but I have not went all the way to see it through." One thing some of these employees appear to need is the knowledge of how to follow through on the process of applying for a transfer. Like the caste-like minorities Ogbu and Matute-Bianchi (1986) describe, some (but not all) of them seem unable (or unwilling) to follow through on their own and want someone to help them along. Their lack of ability (or desire) to act in a way mainstream culture considers appropriate is similar to the child-like behavior some psychoanalysts have suggested is the result of slavery (see Chapter 3). It comes from believing (or recognizing) that there is no possibility for advancement. Thus, many employees accept their current positions as the best the system will allow them to have. They do not see themselves as able to change the system enough to move ahead.

Other employees, however, talk of wanting a better job, transfer-ring to another job, or making more money. But inherent in that desire is the need for knowledge that goes far beyond the portable toolbox of basic skills. At first it is only a glimmer of talk, not well-defined, not spoken, only whispered. But as the program progresses, as the employ-ees feel more comfortable in the classes, and as Aisha works to help them claim their voices, they begin to talk in earnest of why they are willing to leave their jobs for three hours each week to work on tasks that are often seen as "insulting and boring," to risk being harassed by their supervisors, or given no relief in their work load to compensate for the time missed from work.

"Gettin' that piece of paper"

Aisha contributes significantly to the employees' willingness to talk about what they really want. On the first day I observe in the classroom, she acknowledges that many of them are in the classes to improve their skills so they can apply for other jobs in the hospital. But then she pauses and looks at them with quiet intention: "Maybe at King Memorial, but we might have our eyes on a different prize." The prize is related to education and credentials rather than simply to enhanced job skills. In order to understand, let us listen again to Mr. Stone and why he comes to class.

Mr. Stone believes that the most important thing he can do in his life is to earn his GED. He is 38 years old, and was born and raised on a small farm in southern Alabama, the oldest of four children. His broth-er and two sisters have all finished high school and have good jobs. One sister has attended college. But Mr. Stone dropped out in tenth grade. It is not that he did not like school; he just did not have much opportunity to attend. As the oldest, his grandfather expected him to do most of the heavy work around the farm. That meant whenever plowing or plant-ing or harvesting needed to be done, his grandfather made him stay out of school to help. He hated every minute of it. He really enjoyed high school, especially being a member of the marching band. He played all the percussion instruments, and can still set down some mean licks at the lunch table with the silverware. But on the farm, he "didn't learn nothin', except maybe how to be a man."

As soon as he turned 16, he ran away to Chicago to find the father who abandoned him. While in Chicago, he fathered a son of his own whom he has not seen in some time. Returning south to care for his ailing mother and aunt, he left the boy and the boy's mother in Chicago. But while he was gone the mother was murdered, "shot in the face," and the son placed in foster care. Mr. Stone often talks of returning to find his son and bringing him to Bayside, but he always runs into something that prevents him from doing so. He talks about the "system" in Chicago as being too hard to deal with. He is afraid that he will make the long trip and then be unsuccessful in getting custody of his son. He also has a difficult time getting off from work. The financial responsibilities of supporting his mother, aunt, wife, and daughter in Bayside, in addition to paying child support for his son in Chicago keep him working 60 to 80 hours each week. He works 40 hours a week at $5.86 an hour and then does overtime in the emergency room to make up the rest of the money he needs. This ER work, because it has more status than housekeeping, also affords him an added measure of dignity. He works in other areas of the hospital as well and would like to transfer to one of them when he earns his degree. He talks intently of the GED. It is an important symbol. He believes that if he can get it he can do anything, be anything, make twice as much money, only have to work one job instead of two, and maybe get it together enough to go to Chicago and get his boy.

Mr. Stone's work schedule makes it difficult for him to go to night classes and study for the GED test. A few years ago, King Memorial offered GED classes and Mr. Stone took them. He took the test too, although he did not score high enough in any of the areas. (He was only two points away in science.) He still needs to improve his score by about 40 points before he can "get that piece of paper"—the credential he believes will enable him to move out of the margins and into a "good-payin' job."

Mr. Stone's belief in the symbolic power of credentials is an important theme for the employees at King Memorial. Amanda observes the same values in the supervisors' class:

> There is a good deal of talk about the GED. It is a political issue at King Memorial. A person with a GED uses it as a way to pull rank. A person without it wants it, in order to pull rank. I think an ongoing GED class will be very helpful.

Ms. Edwards also wants her GED and is determined to get it:

My new supervisor used to have my job and she admitted she didn't
do it as well as I do, but she went off an' got her GED and started
pullin' herself up. And if she can do it, so can I. I'm not gonna quit
'til I get it.

Ms. Edwards dropped out of school for reasons similar to Mr. Stone's.
She also grew up on a farm, and explains that, "Whenever they got
around to the good stuff in school, we had to stay home and help. And
by the time we got back, all the good stuff was gone." She finally left
school to get married, and the babies came soon after, adding "all them
diapers and all that work." The demands made on her by her husband
and children left her little time to finish her education.

The importance of earning the GED is in possessing the required
credentials—the credentials that make one acceptable in the system.
What becomes increasingly clear as the project unfolds is that at King
Memorial it is impossible to advance from entry level to almost any
other job without a high school diploma or a GED. When Mr. Parrott
objects to Margaret's and Karen's plans to help employees advance at
work, he warns them that it does not happen even when a worker is
qualified. What he fails to mention is that many of his employees are
not considered qualified primarily because they do not possess the required credentials for the job.

When Karen goes to Security to analyze the skills needed for promotion to that department so they can be built into the curriculum, the
supervisor suggests that she is asking the impossible. The requirements
include a GED or high school diploma, a driver's license, a firearms
certificate, and successful completion of a training class. More important, virtually none of the current security staff has been hired from
within King Memorial, and the supervisor tells Karen it is very unlikely
that they will ever hire anyone from the work areas the project is target-
ing. The problem of gatekeeping within the hospital is apparent in the
kinds of requirements necessary to transfer from entry-level jobs in
housekeeping, food service, or laundry to any other form of work. There
are clear divisions between the areas and not a great deal of hope for
crossing over into new areas.

Although there are still employees who want job-specific training
(and who stop attending class when they do not receive it), others hear
about the classes but never actually attend. This group of nonparticip-
ants either say they want GED training and know the classes are not
offering it or say they've had enough of school and do not want any

more. As one woman explains, "I don't need to sit up in no school. I done that already."

Fingeret (1982) has suggested that becoming literate requires a willingness to change one's social relations. Many of these employees are simply unwilling to do so. Others stop coming to class when they realize that their increased literacy skills will change their relationships at home. For example, one woman's boyfriend is quite jealous of her participation even though she is not learning what she had hoped to learn. This jealousy contributes to her dropping out of the classes after the first six weeks. Being part of a community, a social network, is of central importance, and if increasing literacy skills threatens to change that network, then it is not the time to come to class.

On the other hand, Ms. Edwards sees herself as ready for change. She explains that now her children are grown, and she is in a "kind of peaceful place" in her life — ready to reclaim something she lost sight of many years ago. Ms. Edwards looks at her life as a series of cycles. The one she currently sees herself in is the one that affords her the time for learning new things — the season for change. Employees who are most persistent in their participation in the classes are in a place where change is personally possible and does not threaten to disrupt already established patterns of social relations.

"Makin' myself whole"

Earning a GED is symbolically powerful in part because it is not simply a credential for advancement at work, but an acknowledgment of self-worth. For Sarah Rivers, a housekeeping aide, the GED is a symbol of transformation. As she explains to me, "I really want to work on my GED. It's a part of me that's missing that I just got to have and so I never miss class." As she tells me this her voice begins to crack, she coaxes her short grey hair back from her forehead, and wipes tears away with a tissue hidden carefully in the sleeve of her soft blue sweater. Ms. Rivers is disappointed and frustrated when she discovers that the classes do not specifically teach GED skills, but she continues to attend them anyway, and Aisha tries to help her with the GED on the side.

Ms. Rivers wants to be a nurse. In addition to her regular job, she has been doing volunteer work feeding the hospital's elderly patients their meals for quite some time. "I started doing it cause if I didn't some of them old peoples wouldn't even get fed. It hurts me to see it." She feels connected to the babies and older adults she works with at the hospital. Earning a degree so that she can become a fully credentialed caregiver instead of an aide is the prize that motivates her to work so hard.

Thus, Ms. Rivers comes to class eager to learn. She finishes her work early, takes extra work home and is rarely absent. When Aisha gives out the "Weekly Tips" packet, Ms. Rivers finishes it in a few days instead of the six weeks Karen has planned for it to take. Through it all, she talks of needing more out of class, of getting her degree, of making herself whole. Not offering GED training is one of the primary ways the literacy classes fail to meet her needs.

"Lookin' like school"

But advancement and credentials are not the only reasons workers choose to come to class. Many people who have advanced in their work, especially the supervisors, are viewed with dislike or suspicion, so advancement at work does not automatically equate with respect from the community of workers. Many seek improvement for more personal reasons. These men and women enjoy learning in its own right, not as something that will necessarily make them more successful workers. This proves to be one of the most significant ways in which national beliefs and local practice differ. In the 1980s and 1990s, mainstream culture has linked education with jobs. It is commonly believed that what one learns in school helps shape how successful one is in life. And success in life is usually measured by career success. But for the entry-level workers at King Memorial, success is often measured by personal traits rather than occupation, and many highly respected employees appear to have little or no interest in job advancement. For these employees the classes provide an important educational opportunity. They call the classes "school" and act like students. Aisha is the teacher, and they want homework and tests. When they miss class, they talk about "playing hooky." They often discuss with pride their own learning in relation to what their children and grandchildren are learning in school.

That they relate their own work to the schoolwork of their children is particularly interesting, in light of observations made early in the project by both management and some of the center staff that perhaps these employees are having difficulty parenting. As I begin to know them, I develop a different interpretation. Many of the women help their children and grandchildren with homework every night. As a result, they are interested in spelling and math because that is what the children need help with.

Ms. Collins tells me of helping her son with his homework each evening—often he has assignments in all his subjects—and sometimes they stay up until almost 11:00 PM to finish it, no matter how tired she is.

Then she gets up the next morning at 5:00 AM to go to work. This woman does have some difficulty being a single parent, but not because her literacy skills are poor. Rather, her struggle lies in the long, hard hours she works, the standards of care and involvement she has set for herself as a parent, and her lack of material resources. For Ms. Collins, as for many others in the class, traditional education is valued highly. Many of them see themselves as having another opportunity to go to school.

Mr. Fletcher also values school and learning. He is a high school graduate, so he is not in the class for a credential, but because he enjoys being there. He often brings books he has read, and he writes several stories about pivotal events in his life. Mr. Fletcher values learning for its own sake, not as a way to advance at work. At the end of the first six-week session, when Aisha asks each participant to evaluate the class, Mr. Fletcher suggests they do more dictionary work to improve vocabu-lary—maybe a set of words each day. He does not suggest they come from job-related text, but from outside reading materials.

"We're family here"

For the women who have worked at the hospital a long time and do not want to move up themselves, the classes are still important. Having the opportunity to learn more so as to share it with children and grand-children, to make life better for succeeding generations, is very impor-tant. Ms. Taylor tells me she is taking the classes only to learn more math skills. She likes her job and has no desire to move up: "I don't want to go anywhere. At my age, where would I go? I just want to improve my skills so I can help my grandchildrens with their homework." Anoth-er writes: "To learn more out of life and try to be a better person toward my coworkers. To treat people like I want to be treated."

These women tend not to see themselves as separate from their families and coworkers. Rather, they display a highly developed sense of being part of a community of workers who care for and look after one another. The concepts of individual, isolated, contained performance and advancement are generally missing in their talk. When one of the women from housekeeping stops coming to class, she explains her ab-sence this way:

Too much to do. We can't stop cause we have to come to class.
Health, absenteeism, vacation. We can't leave the mens on the
floor. We get ready and team up and do it together. When one person out, we team up and do it. We been there. We just know what
to do.

For many of the women in the class, their connection to their group of coworkers is more important than their own promotion to a new job. Respect is something one achieves within the context of the workplace community, not as the result of individual mobility. The employees who feel most strongly connected to others see the gains of their family and friends as their gains as well.

One good example is Ms. Redding, who works in housekeeping. Ms. Redding has a high school diploma. Soon after she enrolls in the literacy classes, she decides to take the class in medical terminology to qualify for a job in medical records. She passes the class with the second highest score on the test and remarks in class that: "I wanted to be first, but the ambulance driver beat me." Ms. Redding is first in her work, however. She is highly literate, and plays the role of literacy mediator in her department by helping others with everyday literacy needs, such as giving Ms. Thompson the correct spelling of words she needs to write down phone messages at the front desk. When classes are in session, she often spends her lunch hour helping coworkers who are having trouble with their assignments.

Essentially, Ms. Redding reproduces a role she has played all her life. When I ask her why she did not go on to college after high school, she explains: "I'm the oldest of 10 children. I was the second mama. So that's one reason why I didn't go on." She was raised in a small town in Mississippi where she had no access to any form of postsecondary education, so she stayed at home to help with the family until she started a family of her own. In her position as a highly literate employee, Ms. Collins reproduces her role as second mama to other men and women in her department who see themselves as less literate and who rely on her help. She also describes herself as content with this position, and after passing the test decides that her community of friends and her position of respect are more important than a job in medical records, where she would have to start all over as the newest and least skilled employee. Unlike Ms. Edwards and Mr. Stone, she is not interested in changing in her life.

"I wish I could say what I want"

Within this context of community, however, is also a strong pattern of silence, or what Aisha calls "hiding out," the employees' awareness of their lack of ability to speak out—to claim their voices. One of Aisha's recruitment talks for the classes focuses on the improvement of oral communication skills. The center has written this as one of its goals in the grant proposal. As a result, when many of the employees write about why they come to class, they identify improving oral communication skills as a primary goal. Aisha works on this from the very beginning of class, but it is a difficult skill to develop. In part, their lived experiences at work and in the broader community have left many employees feeling defensive and at risk, and this undermines the confidence they need to speak out.

Recall the comment made by Ms. Kelly at the end of the first set of classes (see Chapter 2) about how unfair management is in its hiring practices: "I wish I could speak up, but all I can do is cry and pray. I wish I could say what I want."

In class Aisha helps some of the women become more assertive. For example, she starts having them write real memoranda about things they think are unfair. Ms. Johnson writes and mails a memorandum to the president of the City Council during the final weeks of the class:

> I, Mrs. Janelle Johnson, am writing to you because King Memorial housekeeping staff need more money. If it wasn't for people like me and the laundry and kitchen people, the hospital couldn't run.
>
> We do all the work and we are put down. We are not getting the money we need so we can make way for our families. If the housekeeping staff and the laundry and kitchen staff decided to walk out the hospital couldn't run.
>
> When you are seated at your next board meeting to correct these things please think of the little people at King Memorial.

Ms. Johnson also sends copies of this memorandum to the two mayoral candidates. We never find out whether she receives any reply, but the act of writing it symbolizes a new level of self-confidence for Ms. Johnson, and each class member shares in the pride that goes with her courage.

"This is a story about self-esteem and I don't have any"

During the summer Ms. Benson, one of the food service aides in the class, applies for a job as an anesthesiology technician and wins out over a field of 11 other candidates. She is so happy about her success that she writes an essay for the class describing the process she has gone through to get the job. Aisha uses it as a lesson to teach sequencing and problem solving, but some of the employees are less concerned with the process than with the underlying changes that have to precede any of the steps Ms. Benson says she took to get her new job.

One afternoon as the class is reading the essay, a woman puts her head down on her desk and starts to weep. When Aisha asks her what is wrong, she explains: "This is a story about self-esteem, and I don't have any." Aisha lets her cry for a moment and then softly replies:

> Let us make sure that we also use this as an opportunity to get to the other side of our disappointments, cause we can all be in a room where we can have enough pain to fill up the room, but let's move to the other side of it.

Getting to the other side of the pain is one of the unspoken needs of many of the men and women in the class. And Aisha focuses particularly on this need. She lends her attention to their need for wholeness, their search for lives of hope. For Aisha as well as for the employees, the need is much more basic than the ability to sequence a task or read a chart, the need is to live a decent life.

It would be simplistic, however, to assume that all employees lack self-esteem. Some of the men and women in the classes believe they have already realized that goal, even while holding the most humble of jobs. Ms. Wallace, a housekeeping aide, writes this essay about her work:

> Working in the Housekeeping department is very interesting. You get to meet many people in all walks of life: doctors, nurses, foreign people, and many patients. You also learn to communicate with the public. You learn to think of your job as a talent. You learn how to clean with dignity and honor. Although I will like very much to move up, I'm still proud of my job as a Housekeeping Aide.

Aisha's Goals:
"We need to give them the gift of something they want"

Aisha resists the functional context approach to the teaching of literacy because she believes that the goals of the program are exploitive and inappropriate. She is critical of many of the categorizations made about the employees and their needs. As the program progresses, she becomes more and more critical of its assumptions and its goals.

"It needs to look like school"

Although Margaret argues that school has let workers down by not teaching them what they need to survive in the workplace, Aisha believes that education and credentials are still very important symbols in the Black community. She mentions that the attraction the ministry has for many Black men is its validation by way of the credential earned. Giddings writes of the value of education for Blacks in the years after the Civil War in *When and Where I Enter* (1984), Aisha's favorite history of the contributions of Black women to American history:

> Going to school was considered important for both men and women and essential for the latter. . . . No matter what their thirst for knowledge, it was particularly important for women to get an education because the majority of them had to work. (pp. 104–105)

Giddings explains that education protected the men and women at their work rather than guaranteed their advancement. Thus within the Black community, education has been tied not only to advancement, but to protection, to status, to respect.

The goals of the literacy program, tied so heavily to productivity and advancement, do not fit the goals and values of many members of the Black community at King Memorial. For example, Aisha takes exception to Margaret's belief that the employees will not like the classes if they look like school. She maintains that it shows how little Margaret and the center staff "know about the culture."

For example, unlike the ALRC staff, Aisha is especially concerned with the spelling, grammar, and punctuation of a writing assignment. In the beginning of the project Karen discovers that Aisha is correcting the employees' writing for spelling, punctuation, and grammar rather than focusing on the content. Karen becomes concerned that Aisha is going to "undermine the very skills she has been hired to develop." Karen believes writing instruction should emphasize process and is critical of Aisha's "overemphasis" on the surface features. At one point she begins to think that Aisha does not understand how to teach literacy skills. Aisha dismisses Karen's concerns as another example of White teachers not understanding what Black people want and need to learn.

The employees confirm that they want to know more about words — about spelling and handwriting, about making things correct, making them look right. As with their jobs, they value their class work when it looks good. Appearance and correctness are sources of dignity and pride. The way something looks upon completion is more central than the process one goes through to get it to look that way. At the end of the classes, Ms. Edwards is as proud of the improvement in her hand writing as she is in her improved reading skills.

This concern with correctness and with appearances has been remarked on by other Black teachers of Black students. Delpit concludes, from her work with inner-city Black schoolchildren, that for these students, correctness in form and mechanics is valued because they believe they must know these skills to be successful in school (1986). Jordan found the same thing when she assigned *The Color Purple* in a class of mostly Black college students. Her students were confused and angry that she would assign something that "looked funny." So although employees resist the curriculum developed from job skills, they also resist a purely process approach to teaching writing. They want to know the "right" way to spell a word or shape a letter. Their class work has to "look good" before they are satisfied with it.

There are other ways in which Aisha believes the project is not geared to the needs of Black employees. She says that it is a tradition in the Black community not to teach children that education will automatically lead to advancement because, she says, "for many of us, it hasn't." Rather, she believes education should be tied to self-improvement in more general terms, learning for the sake of learning, not for the sake of working.

These beliefs of Aisha's are echoed in the work of Foster (1989), who has studied educators the Black community defines as successful in educating its children. One of the common themes running through Foster's work is the teachers' belief that they must teach Black children that school does not necessarily lead to advancement. Instead, they believe Black children must learn to value education in its own right, not simply as a ticket for a good job.

In the final analysis, Aisha believes the workplace literacy program is exploitive, simplistic, and culturally insensitive—"a reflection of the narrowness of the military mind." As she observes on more than one occasion, "I just don't like the politics."

The Hidden Curriculum

As a result of Aisha's very basic differences with the rest of the center staff, she soon develops what she labels the "hidden curriculum" to resist the implications of functional education and teach what she thinks the employees really need to learn. She talks of layering the lessons with her own issues, issues she calls "real."

One of her first assignments is the *Raisin in the Sun* lesson. In addition, she brings her friends who are visiting from Belize (where plantations still operate) to talk about their country's politics and culture. She tells the employees about the shop in Bayside that sells African artifacts, pottery, waist beads, and baskets—a place none of them have ever visited. She talks about the need of young Black women and men to claim their African heritage and describes how to cook collard greens in a wok with a little ginger and no fatback. She introduces them to Alice Walker and Byllye Avery, to the poetry of Langston Hughes and the politics of health care for African-Americans. She hopes to take the class on a field trip to Atlanta at the end of the project to visit the Apex Museum and Martin Luther King's tomb, a place many of them have never seen. All of these things are part of the "possible," part of what she thinks employees need to know.

Center staff knows what Aisha is doing in class. She talks about it and writes some of it in her lesson plans as well. They are not as enthusiastic about the eclectic curriculum as she is. Aisha's lessons might be interesting—even politically "correct," but they are not the workplace literacy the funding agency is sponsoring. However, Aisha also includes many assignments that more closely match grant objectives. She teaches innumerable lessons on sequencing and learning vocabulary words from work-related text. She includes the lessons Karen develops, such as the one on how to read a pay stub, but she calls some lessons "deadly" and finishes them quickly so she can move on to other topics.

Often, if no one else is in the class as a "spy," she teaches GED materials, and she convinces several employees to take the test. She has them "partner together" to support one another through the experience. Ms. Stevens has a friend come over early one Saturday morning and take her to the GED testing center. She says she would never have had the courage to try again without the help of her partner and the support of the class. As with many other things, Aisha works with the GED curriculum to enhance the sense of community already present for many of the workers.

"Being in the world"

Aisha believes that the employees need not only to improve their reading and writing skills but also to develop the self-confidence to assert themselves, to realize a vision of the possible in their lives. For her, this is what workplace literacy should be about, not meeting the needs of the employer or the needs of the government, but helping workers examine the sociopolitical context of their lives and determine what they need to "be in the world." She encourages workers to reject any notion of caste-like minority status and to develop a belief in a future of possibility.

Her notions about employees' literacy needs match those of many of the class members as well. Here is the class evaluation Mr. Fletcher writes at the end of the project. Notice his emphasis on confidence and self-esteem as well as on improving his interpersonal skills. However, it is also possible to interpret the essay as a support of Margaret's claims that workers do not learn anything of importance in school, and that learning basic skills enhances self-esteem. How one interprets Mr. Fletcher's essay depends in part on how one reads the world as well as how one reads the word.

LOOKING THROUGH MY CLASS FOLDER

The papers most meaningful to me, in my folder are the essays, and my letter of resignation. The essays, because they are very stimulating to the mind, and with the instructor's encouragement is a lot of fun. The letters of resignation and transfer request are very meaningful, too. I might be writing one soon. Who knows? Its good to have some knowledge about business letters.

Thanks to the wonderful instructors, I have learned a lot of helpful and meaningful things in class. The job enhancement course has given me so much confidence, and self esteem. Working and communicating better with my co-workers.

I didn't learn anything in high school, and it is not all my fault. I believe it is mostly the teachers and the system's fault. Thank you (instructors) very much for teaching me to value my mind, and giving me the incentive of wanting to learn again. That is why I did not drop out, and stayed to the end. I'm now thinking about some night classes. Wish me luck.

The classes Mr. Fletcher plans to take are art and photography. Although they are not related to his work, they are the very things he mentions in his essay in the prologue: "My hobbies are photography, drawing & painting, when the mood hit me. Lately that ain't been too often." Evidently, something about the classes put him in the mood to once more pursue favorite talents, things that give him pleasure and a sense of accomplishment, things not at all related to the work he does each day at the hospital.

When the project is being developed, center staff members hold beliefs about employee literacy needs based on Margaret's advice and the growing public discourse on workplace literacy. After several months of working with employees, hearing their stories, and learning about their lives, a somewhat different picture of their needs and values begins to take shape.

In general, the men and the women in the classes want to increase their sense of self-worth, their self-esteem. For many of them this means a better job with more status and more money. But the process for getting that job is perceived by employees to be more complex than simply improving their skills. For several of them it means getting a GED first, and then trying for another job. But for quite a few, the first step is to develop effective communication skills, to find a voice, and to have the courage to use it — to move beyond the resignation of being stuck on the bottom. Others do not want to advance at work, but want to help others in their family accomplish their goals. Helping children and grandchildren with homework is an important reason for attending classes. Learning simply for the sake of learning is also important for many.

Other employees never come to class, or drop out after a few classes because they are not interested in what the classes offer. Either the curriculum is not tied enough to getting the GED, or there is no opportunity to learn the skills for a new and very different job from the one they currently hold. Still other employees choose not to participate because they do not want to change.

Aisha perceives the literacy needs of the employees differently from either the center staff and consultants or the employees. She wants to reshape the goals and definitions of the project to be more responsive to what she believes to be the needs of employees. The center staff, however, feels tightly bound to upholding the guidelines of the funding agency. They have taken its money, and they are obligated to perform within its guidelines.

Aisha, however, is more focused on employees' concept of self, teaching them to help themselves, and encouraging them to think critically, to change the system. She develops a number of lessons that are not directly related to the workplace, and the center staff is concerned that she does not know how to teach literacy skills properly. She also develops a series of lessons on GED materials that she gives out quietly as homework because center staff knows GED training is not what the program has been funded to teach.

When the King Memorial project draws to a close, Noreen and Rose set about assessing the outcomes of the project and writing a final report. At the same time, I begin intense postfield data analysis to write up my own final report. We do not share our different interpretations. Aisha is not asked to write a final report of her own, but she does so anyway. All these assessments consider the program from different perspectives. The next chapter reviews these different interpretations of the same program and offers suggestions for recognizing the multiple, cooccurring literacies that create the fabric of workplace life.

CHAPTER 7

Assessing Outcomes

In September, when the Work Skills Development Program at King Memorial Hospital officially ends, Noreen and Rose set out to assess the outcomes of the project for the final report, and Karen begins to write a curriculum guide to be used in other programs. The King Memorial project is assessed in a variety of ways. This book represents one interpretation of the project. Other players, given their assigned roles from inception, make other choices for assessment.

The Center's Assessment

The center, as part of the funding agency's requirements, develops a detailed program evaluation. It is based on a variety of measures including statistics, structured interviews, oral communication evaluations, and writing samples. The assessment concludes that employees show gains in reading, writing, and oral communication, but only those gains in oral communication are statistically significant. From the interview data, the report concludes that the increase in oral communication skills is also linked to an increase in self-confidence, especially in expressing opinions about work-related matters. These outcomes are described as having an "indirect" benefit to the hospital. The final report goes on to explain that the program is too short-lived to help employees actually realize their job and educational objectives, and urges continued funding for the project. Unfortunately, the program is not funded for another cycle nor does the hospital institutionalize the program, so employees who have started to improve their literacy skills are left to find other instruction on their own time.

Karen finds writing the curriculum guide difficult. Her heart is not in the project. She concludes that the ingredients in the project that have contributed most highly to its success are the "personal aspects" that Aisha has contributed.

Aisha's Assessment

Aisha makes her own personal assessment of the project, but does not contribute to the center's final report. During the last weeks of classes, she enters the hospital for major surgery and is unable to return to work. Strained feelings between herself and the center staff make further communications difficult. Her actions are seen as undermining the program, and her analysis is not included in the final evaluation. She believes she has been made invisible and voiceless by White women who outrank her academically. She makes repeated requests for her notes and papers to be forwarded to her, but does not receive them for quite some time. Much later, and for a different audience, she gives a talk describing her own interpretation of what happened in the project. A full transcription of that talk appears below:

> I am Aisha R. Samara, the workplace literacy project's "instructional coordinator"—the teacher. This is *my* final report—my sense of what occurred—my summing up—my story of the workers who were involved from King Memorial Hospital. This is my story about me and my colleagues from Bayside University's Adult Literacy Research Center. My story, our story, now your story about who we are, what this workplace literacy project was, how it worked, and more importantly, how we worked despite it.
>
> It is a Tuesday/Wednesday/Thursday, January–September, 1989. My supervisor has picked me, or I've picked myself to come to this thing—these classes they're calling work skills development. A Black woman showed up at our early morning employees' meeting to talk to us, have us sign on. Some of us actually made it. Some of us, even though we signed up, never got to go! Supervisor says he needs us to work, or I need to understand this is a reward.
>
> Classes are for six weeks. There'll be math, something they call critical thinking and problem solving, and there'll be reading. I always wanted to improve my reading, especially understanding what I've read and spelling words correctly.
>
> School starts. This *is* school for me, with desks, a blackboard, and a teacher. I want books. I ride the elevator until she starts talking about walking up the stairs is good for my heart. How come she doesn't understand I walk millions of miles throughout this big old hospital all day long?
>
> Here I come. I wear my pink, white, or green uniform or I change to street dress and wear high heels. I am 18 to 65, single mother of one, grandmother of six, a father taking care of mother,

aunt, children, and sister. I have been at the Kings for 15 years, 20 years, 30 years. I completed the third grade, the fourth, the six, the tenth, the eleventh, or the twelfth. I want my GED. This is a way to get it, isn't it? Why else should I come? Or do I want to knock the rust off of this old brain?

Who else has been picked to attend? Did their coworkers tease them, laugh and call them illiterate, or did they encourage them like the nurses did me? Did their daughters say "Go ahead, mom, you can do it"? Did their husband fight them for going to a school for "dummies"? Who's in here with me? Mainly my coworkers from the laundry, or housekeeping, or the kitchen. I knew her, I knew him, grandmother, mother of children who won't leave home. Parents of adult children sick with kidney disease. When we tell our stories, the teacher takes our health profile. We have asthma, hypertension, seizures of an unexplained nature, heart disease, lupus, and arthritis.

We have military experience. Children in the military in Germany and England, where we've never visited. We've been dishwashers, baby-sitters, day workers, hotel maids. We've mothered too early and too long, still keeping our grandchildren in our homes even as we near retirement.

Finally I'm in the classroom. I tell my story, introduce myself, write my story, but not before I take the test. She calls it an assessment. My hands shake as I reach for the pencil she gives me after she hands out this assessment. I plead, "Let me get my glasses, get water, have more time," wipe my sweating hands on my uniform and next day I don't return or return scared. I know a test when I've taken one.

I am Aisha R. Samara, a Black woman recruited for the workplace literacy project. What a challenge this is. Did they pick me based on my work in community-based education and training or for my work in health advocacy/community organizing? From the outset they speak to each other in our meetings—looking to each other for confirmation of themselves, a meeting of equals in their minds. I pledge not to buy in to the split between academia and the community being played out in microcosm. We do not agree.

Sure they may want a GED but it misleads them. Do not correct language, their spelling. We're not doing that. (We're not?) That empowerment stuff is all right, but it won't work in this applied research program.

We as a people have always operated out of an acknowledged dualism. Why should this be any different? I begin my closed-door curriculum. I set up shop outside of their classroom, the one they've conceptualized, the project that emerged from their sense of what's possible.

I construct instead a parallel curriculum that is deployed only when we're alone and the door is closed. This is not built on the jobs they are presently involved in but the ones they want and to earn the GED. These are the prizes that they have their eyes on.

We talk about the person: empowerment, self-esteem, health, staying emotionally well, financially stable, housing, our culture. I cry too when my sister breaks down in the middle of class and cries, "Nobody ever encouraged me to do this before."

We work our way through the months. Some continue, most cannot, having to make room for others. I read excerpts from Black books, personal letters from friends from Africa, bring in friends from Central America and southwest Africa. We watch television shows, recommend movies and videos, make up work sheets for grandchildren who came to class with grandmother, and talk to older children, providing information and applications for college. We call folks at home, send notes of condolence for the workers whose mothers, fathers, uncles, and aunts die, whose 18-year-old grandson dies of a brain tumor.

I visit them at work. The intent is for me to know them well enough to use their real aspirations to construct a real curriculum: understanding your paycheck, word problems, reading, editing their own stories, sending memos to the mayor, and taking the GED. Tutors come in and strengthen the work providing sorely needed one-on-one even as we encourage partnering, calling each other, checking on each other at work. They call me at home with homework, introduce me to friends when I meet them in the cafeteria or downtown.

We merge even as I learn to know them as individuals in not just their needs but in what their longings are. I have learned some things from them, we have learned some things from each other. I thank them all for being my teachers.

How a program is assessed depends on how we choose to listen to the voices of all the players, which ones to emphasize, which ones to downplay, which ones we perhaps inadvertently ignore. Some of those choices are conscious; others are bounded by closely held, often unexamined beliefs about knowledge and power. The various assessments of the literacy program described here are examples of the possible variety of conclusions to be drawn from the same project. The questions we seek to answer determine the assessments we conduct. The ways in which we find the answers, in turn, often shape the final conclusions of the assessment. As a result, the King Memorial project has been described in a variety of ways in the literature that has been generated about it. My own intention has been to listen to those who are rarely involved in assessment as they speak about their own interpretations of the workplace literacy program in which they participate. Thus, the conclusions I draw about the program must be taken as my own interpretations of a specific project — a project contextualized in a given moment of time in a particular region of the country. I claim no generalizability for this study. Rather, the story this book tells is the unfolding of one literacy initiative — the attitudes, activities, and processes that shape it and the constraints in which it is carried out. Its significance lies in readers' conceptions of literacy, competence, and work as well as their valuation of workers' conceptions of these same issues.

Workplace Literacy and Change

For those readers hopeful that workplace literacy might serve as a catalyst for social and economic change, it is important to consider the broader contexts in which these programs are situated. One way to develop this broader understanding is to use ethnographic techniques to develop an interpretive understanding of the ecology of literacy: the values and uses of language and text in the lives of all the participants in the project — from entry-level employees to top management. (See Heath, 1982, for a description of such a model to investigate literacy in communities and schools. My own suggestions are based on her guidelines.)

On the surface, this process might appear similar to the functional context approach recommended for the King Memorial project. In fact, literacy audits and ethnographic inquiry employ similar methods of data collection: participant observation, interviews, and the collection of artifacts. What differs are the theoretical frameworks that guide the two methodologies. In Margaret's functional context approach, for example, one assumes there is a portable toolbox of basic skills that is embedded in job tasks and that can be uncovered, made explicit, and then taught to all employees — a universal set of skills that applies across jobs and people and social structures. In an ethnographic approach, on the other hand, one is looking for an understanding of the ways literacy is socially constructed within and across the various groups that constitute the community of workers in a specific workplace. In this instance, it is assumed that literacy will be different for different people in different situations. Cultural and social differences are expected and acknowledged rather than taken as signs of deficit.

An ethnographic approach includes multiple methods of observations, questions, and collection procedures. The researcher collects print materials and observes the ways workers interact (or avoid interaction) with these materials. The contexts of these interactions, including the use of time and space, are important aspects to include in these observations. The observer also notes the ways in which these artifacts are displayed to workers.

The norms for literacy are also carefully observed. Who produces text, and who uses it? When is oral communication favored over written communication to convey information? How are written materials used? How is literacy valued by various in-groups? How is literacy acquisition related to credentials? What are the purposes of writing text (to describe, to define, to control)? And what are the purposes of reading texts (information, self-improvement, pleasure)?

Most important, how is the workplace structured? How much effort in the workplace is related to boundary maintenance, and how is literacy used toward those ends? Unlike communities or schools that are often treated as individual units of analysis, workplaces generally contain a combination of smaller in-groups with different uses for and beliefs about literacy. It is important to identify and study each of these in-groups and their relationships to one another in order to understand the complexity of the work organization and the ways literacy fits into the structure.

Finally, it is important to understand the broader social and historical contexts of the community in which the workplace is located. This kind of ethnographic research could lead to a richer understanding of particular workplace organizations and to the development of comprehensive literacy programs appropriate for the variety of individuals and groups that make up the organization. In this way, we could also begin to understand the process of change inherent in literacy education and how it affects and is affected by the broader structures in which it is situated.

In the King Memorial project, workplace literacy is conceived as a narrowly defined solution to a wide range of problems. It overlooks the social and political contexts of the lives of entry-level workers and interprets their behaviors as signs of poor literacy and problem solving skills. This, in turn, serves to both justify and perpetuate their positions as entry-level workers. Poor literacy skills are seen as threatening to the workplace and a detriment to the economic and social well-being of the country. Entry-level workers are characterized as confused, incapable of problem solving, parenting, or performing with competence on the job. The ways that these women and men actually do live in the world belie these myths.

It appears, however, that the agenda for literacy training may not be to increase literacy skills but to alter behavior to more closely match mainstream culture. Karen eventually decides that this is the real agenda in the King Memorial project. A few months after the project starts, she complains to Margaret:

> *Karen:* If we really reduce the message we get from the Lewises or Parrotts, it doesn't matter what color the Lewis or the Parrott is, the bottom line message is, what we don't like in our workers, whether they're front-line supervisors or entry-level workers, we don't like them acting like the Black lower class. We don't like them—even if they *do* use the forms, as these front line supervisors *do*—if they have a grammatical error that reflects . . . non-standard . . . dialect. Or, if they handle a problem like a lower class, or maybe a person from a more— uh, I don't know how to word this. The real message is not we want them to fill out these forms better. The real message is we want them to be different human beings. [To Amanda, who helped her interview management a second time for a supervisors' class] Did you hear that?
>
> *Amanda:* Yeah. I don't know that I'd say it that strongly. They wanted them to be middle class. Have a different attitude toward everything.
>
> *Karen:* That's where my frustration comes in. Because we literally asked Parrott to show us some reprimands, and yes, they followed the form. And these supervisors can tell you rules. They really can. They know what their management wants. But, you know, they don't deliver it in the voice, with the verbal language . . . I'm saying this because it doesn't break down to race because Harvey Parrott is a Black man—wants it just as much.
>
> *Aisha:* More.
>
> *Karen:* Yeah, more. That's something I've been frustrated about.

When workplace literacy training is an effort to initiate minority and working class employees into mainstream ways of communication and behavior, resistance is an understandable response. When literacy providers uncritically accept this agenda and focus only on skills, little significant long term change will occur.

A more productive approach would be to adopt a participatory model of workplace education. This model would invite all stakeholders to the table to mutually determine both the problem and its possible solutions (see Fisher & Ury, 1981 and Whyte, 1991 for examples of the theoretical frameworks and mediation techniques that enhance employee participation in the decision-making process). It is within a participatory model that literacy training in the workplace has the best chance for significant change. By necessity, this model will create new ways for participants to see their situations. And it calls upon the literacy educator to abandon the role of expert and to assume the role of facilitator — to abandon notions of deficit and to search instead for the abilities already constituted in workers but often unrecognized by institutions or assessment measures.

Most importantly it calls upon literacy educators to recognize that all of us possess our own illiteracies — especially our inability to recognize competence and skill in the Other. Perhaps the mark of a truly literate person in a complex society is the ability to recognize and value more than one's own ways of knowing. Perhaps the mark of truly literate educators and managers is the ability to incorporate these differences into more humane, democratic, and rewarding workplaces.

Epilogue

Two years after the conclusion of the King Memorial project, I return to Bayside to visit Mr. Stone, Ms. Edwards, and the other employees I have come to know during this study. I wonder what has happened in the two years since the employees have had access to a formal literacy program on work time. What I find is both discouraging and hopeful.

For most of the program participants, little change can be seen in their material circumstances or in their job positions. A few of them have tried to continue attending some sort of program on their own, but this has not been easy.

Mr. Stone has been taking GED classes sporadically at the local high school two evenings a week. As a result he has not made as much money as he used to, and "things are really tight." He continues to attend his church and to study the Bible daily. He still works for Ms. Butler, and still resents her treatment of him. Ms. Butler thinks he is "too proud" to work in housekeeping and wishes he could find some other job in the hospital. So far, he has been unsuccessful in doing so.

Ms. Edwards has been transferred to another work area where she has weekends off. She is happier with this job, but she still has not received a promotion because she still has not been able to earn her GED. She goes to school at night sometimes, but like Mr. Stone, she attends intermittently. She tells me that when she finds a teacher she likes, the program is canceled or the teacher is reassigned to another class. So far she has been unable to find a program that suits her. She is also rather bitter about the literacy classes and what she has learned from them. She explains that "no one cares about us little peoples. No one is going to help me do it. I've stopped worrying about those other folks. I'm just going to have to look out for me." She has no interest in continuing to work together with other employees from her class as partners. She sees herself as alone in her struggle to achieve her goals. The classes she attends encourage her to go on, but they also change her interpretation of how she fits into the economic and social structure at work. Not one of the program participants has earned a GED. Two employees who already have high school diplomas have managed to earn job promotions.

Ms. Benson is one of the two employees to advance to a better job after attending the literacy classes. She continues to enjoy her work as an anesthesiology technician. She is enthusiastic about what Aisha taught her — the self-confidence and determination to go on and a belief in the possible. Ms. Moore, who works in the sewing room of the laundry, has also earned a promotion as a result of Aisha's encouragement and help. Ms. Moore finally gained the self-confidence to believe she deserved a better job with a better salary, and so Aisha helped her draft a request for a promotion and pay raise. Ms. Moore's request was honored, and she is now a supervisor making much better money for her work.

Ms. Kelly is retiring early with disability due to the injury to her hand. She is hoping to attend GED classes now that she no longer works during the day. Earning her GED is a personal goal rather than something to enable her to advance at work. She stays very busy with her church and the community center it sponsors. She describes the church as a central part of her life, and the sense of community it offers is an important aspect of her happiness. When she retires, the personnel department of the hospital, as they do for all retiring employees, sponsors a reception for her with plenty of food, a piano player, formal invitations, and a speech from one of the managers in the personnel department. Ms. Kelly wears a red dress with matching shoes. All her children and grandchildren are there, dressed in their Sunday best. Her minister attends and makes a short speech describing how much Ms. Kelly has contributed to the church and how important she is to the community.

Mr. Fletcher continues to work as a group leader in the housekeeping department under Ms. Butler. He wishes the hospital had an art gallery to display the employees' work. He believes there are many others like himself who have creative talents that could be displayed in the hospital. He continues with his art and photography, but has no plans to make any changes in his position at work.

Although the lives of the men and women in this study seem to have changed very little, the hospital has undergone several dramatic changes. First, the renovations so long argued about on the county level have been approved and are beginning. Some buildings are being gutted and renovated; others buildings are now designated for new uses. One of these is the building where Mr. Stone and Mr. Fletcher work. During the conversion from dormitory to office space, the furniture is moved out and stored in another building, then moved back to the building from which it originally came. Mr. Fletcher and Mr. Stone spend many long hot days moving heavy furniture around the hospital grounds just to see it returned again to its original building while the management decides whether to store it or sell it or give it away.

Meanwhile, in the parking lot where Mr. Stone found his watch, there is now a Burger King. When the hospital agreed to let the restaurant open a franchise on the property, the local newspaper ran a story. A reporter interviewed Mr. Lewis, the director of food services, asking him what he thought about fast food being served on the hospital premises. He said he didn't think it mattered much, because people were going to eat the stuff anyway, so why not to make it accessible to them.

Another, more sweeping change is taking place at King Memorial. The chief administrative officer has been replaced. The new administrator, Mr. Harris, is a Black man from an urban hospital up North. In the two years he has been in charge, significant changes have been made. Many of the staff employed in the personnel department during the literacy program are no longer there. They have left for other positions or have been transferred to night duty. In addition, Mr. Harris has hired a woman to head up an HRD program. He has told her specifically that evaluations of employee performance will be changed, that employees will no longer be blocked from promotion, that GED and literacy classes will become part of the training available to all employees, and that persons who stand in the way of these changes will be dealt with severely. In short, the very structures that made it so difficult to effect real change through literacy classes are now being reorganized with a new administrator. It is too early to see how these changes will be implemented and to what extent they will affect the lives of the employees who see themselves as stuck in their jobs. But the future looks a bit more hopeful than it did two years ago.

Others have been touched by the King Memorial program, and their stories also fit into this final review. Noreen continues to run the Adult Literacy Research Center. The grant monies the center has won now total over $2 million. The literacy program was recently given favorable reviews by an outside assessment team, which strengthens Noreen's chances of earning more grant money. Karen no longer works at the center. She has returned to teaching and writing full time. In addition, she has recently been awarded a large grant to study the requirements of academic literacy for beginning college students. She has won tenure and promotion in part due to her original workplace grant. Rose has changed the focus of her doctoral work from secondary education to adult literacy training in the workplace. She hopes to find work as a consultant in the field once she graduates.

My own life has changed dramatically as a result of this study. Of course, the most obvious changes are professional. I have graduated, given several papers on my work, written articles for publication, and completed this book as well — my experience with the King project has given me valuable new knowledge and significant professional reward. But the changes go much deeper than that. I have also lost a certain trust in the institutions that have shaped my life. This includes not only the university and its relationship to funding agencies, but also my church and the social networks of which I have been a part.

My children and husband have also changed. Living with the King project was a dramatic and often painful experience for all of us and has brought our own values into a sharper focus. We are all more deeply concerned with current economic and social policy, and more sensitive to the racism and classism woven into the fabric of our daily lives.

But this critical awareness brings with it a risk of cynicism, and cynicism accomplishes very little. It co-opts employees' stories and reduces them to fit our own political agendas. Consider, for example, this note that Ms. Dyson wrote to Aisha at the end of the project:

> Aisha, you are the first black woman teacher that encourage me. Didn't say anything to let me down. You always said, "Come on, you can do it." I thank you for pushing me to do better. Also learn me about black women writers that I enjoy learning about. I have gone far in life. I am reading better, my spelling is a little better. Thank you so much for being here for me.

Without the King project, Ms. Dyson and Aisha would have never met, and this note of thanks would never have been written.

I would also like to suggest that even in programs that are less than exemplary, there is the possibility to initiate important institutional change. This happened as a result of the King project as well. Noreen and Amanda have designed and implemented a worker-centered literacy program for Bayside University staff that focuses specifically on the third-shift workers in the physical plant. Success in securing funding for the King project and positive evaluations from the funding agency have served to convince the university administration that ALRC can assist in offering an important opportunity for workers who, like those at King Memorial, are on the margins, providing work vital to the institution's very existence, yet sharing in very few of its rewards.

I could close this book by reflecting on the conflicts, limitations, arrogance, and insensitivity that occurred (most often unintentionally) during the King project. We could take the stories I have told as evidence of institutional ineptness or even maliciousness. But I suggest we do not. Instead I would like to think of the King project in another way: as an important event that offers us stories about literacy, about work, and about ourselves—stories that may be of help shaping other programs to more closely fit employee needs and abilities. When I ask the workers at King Memorial if I can share their stories, they most generously agree. They ask me to tell these stories so that others might begin to hear and see—so that policy makers and program planners might begin to weave new understandings of the diversity, integrity, and skill of the American worker. This book is an attempt to honor that request.

References

A nation at risk: The imperative for educational reform. (1983). Washington, DC: National Commission on Excellence in Education.

Action for excellence. (1983). Denver, CO: Education Commission of the United States.

Adelman, C. (1991). *Women at thirtysomething: Paradoxes of attainment* (DOE publication no. OR 91-530). Washington, DC: U.S. Government Printing Office.

Anderson, J. D. (1988). *The education of Blacks in the South, 1860-1935.* Chapel Hill, NC: University of North Carolina Press.

Baldwin, J. (1988). If Black English isn't a language, then tell me, what is? In C. Muscatine & M. Griffith (Eds.), *The Borzoi college reader*, 6th ed. (pp. 162-165). New York: Knopf. (Reprinted from *New York Times*, 29 July 1979)

Bartlett, I. H., & Cambor, C. G. (1974). The history and psychodynamics of southern womanhood. *Women's Studies, 2*, 9-24.

Belenky, M., Clinchy, B., Goldberger, J., & Tarule, J. (1986). *Women's ways of knowing.* New York: Basic Books.

Boss, V. (1990). Personal communication.

The bottom line: Basic skills in the workplace. (1988). Washington, DC: U.S. Departments of Education and Labor.

Carnevale, A. P., Gainer, L. J., & Meltzer, A. S. (1990). *Workplace basics: The essential skills employers want.* San Francisco: Jossey Bass.

Carnevale, A., Gainer, L. J., & Meltzer, A. (no date). *Workplace basics: The skills employers want.* Washington, DC: Employment & Training Administration, U.S. Department of Labor.

Chisman, F. P. (1989). *Jumpstart: The federal role in adult literacy.* Southport, CT: Southport Institute of Policy Analysis.

Cohen, A. (1991). Personal communication.

Cohen, R. A. (1969). Conceptual styles, culture conflict, and nonverbal tests of intelligence. *American Anthropologist, 71*(5), 828-856.

Cook-Gumperz, J. (1986). Introduction: The social construction of literacy. In J. Cook-Gumpertz (Ed.), *The social construction of literacy* (pp. 1-15). New York: Cambridge University Press.

Cornell, T. (1988). Characteristics of effective occupational literacy programs. *Journal of Reading, 31*(7), 654-657.

de Castell, S., & Luke, A. (1988). Defining "literacy" in North American schools. In E. R. Kintgen, B. M. Kroll & M. Rose (Eds.), *Perspectives on literacy* (pp. 159–174). Carbondale, IL: Southern Illinois University Press.

Delpit, L. (1986). Skills and other dilemmas of a Black educator. *Harvard Educational Review*, 56(4), 379–385.

DeMarco, T. (1990, November-December). Forecasting a sea-change. *Human Capital*, pp. 15–18.

Diehl, W., & Mikulecky, L. (1980). The nature of reading at work. *Journal of Reading*, 24(3), 221–227.

Educating America for the twenty-first century. (1983). Washington, DC: National Science Board.

Elkins, S. M. (1978). *Slavery: A problem in American institutional and intellectual life* (3rd. ed.). Chicago: Univeristy of Chicago Press.

Erickson, F. (1988). School literacy, reasoning and civility: An anthropologist's perspective. In E. R. Kintgen, B. M. Kroll & M. Rose (Eds.), *Perspectives on literacy* (pp. 205–226). Carbondale, IL: Southern Illinois University Press.

Fingeret, A. (1982). *The illiterate underclass: Demythologizing an American stigma*. Unpublished doctoral dissertation, Syracuse University, Syracuse, NY.

Fisher, R. & Ury, W. (1981). *Getting to yes: Negotiating agreement without giving in*. New York: Penguin Books.

Fitzhugh, G. (1960). *Cannibals all! or slaves without masters*. Cambridge, MA: Belnap Press.

Fitzhugh, G. (1965). *Sociology for the south, or the failure of free society*. New York: Burt Franklin.

Fordham, S., & Ogbu, J. (1986). Black students' school success: Coping with the burden of "acting white." *The Urban Review*, 18(3), 176–195.

Foster, M. (1989, January). *Just got to find a way: Afro-Americans speak about their lives as teachers*. Paper presented at the Qualitative Research in Education meeting, Athens, Georgia.

Fox-Genovese, E. (1988). *Within the plantation household*. Chapel Hill, NC: University of North Carolina Press.

Fox-Genovese, E. (1991). *Feminism without illusions*. Chapel Hill, NC: University of North Carolina Press.

Freire, P., & Macedo, D. (1987). *Literacy: Reading the word and the world*. South Hadley, ME: Bergin & Garvey.

Gawthrop, R. (1987). Literacy drives in pre-industrial Germany. In R. F. Arnove & H. J. Graff (Eds.), *National literacy campaigns: Historical and comparative perspectives* (pp. 29–48). New York: Plenum Press.

Genovese, E. (1967). Rebelliousness and docility in the negro slave. *Civil War History*, 13(4), 293–314.

Giddings, P. (1984). *When and where I enter*. New York: Bantam Books.

Gilligan, C. (1982). *In a different voice*. Cambridge, MA: Harvard University Press.

Giroux, H. A. (1983). *Theory and resistance in education*. South Hadley, MA: Bergin & Garvey.

Goodman, K. S., Goodman, Y. M., & Hood, W. J. (1989). *The whole language evaluation book*. Portsmouth, NH: Heinemann.

Graff, H. (1979). *The literacy myth: Literacy and social structure in the 19th century city*. New York: Academic Press.

Graff, H. (1987). *The labyrinths of literacy*. New York: Falmer Press.

Greenacre, P. (1947). Child wife as ideal: Sociological consideration. *American Journal of Orthopsychiatry, 17*, 167–171.

Harper, W. (1853). *The pro-slavery argument*. Philadelphia: Lippincott, Grambo.

Heath, S. B. (1982). Ethnography in education: Defining the essentials. In P. Gilmore & A. Glatthorn (Eds.), *Children in and out of school*. Washington, DC: Center for Applied Linguistics.

Heath, S. B. (1983). *Ways with words: Language, life, and work in communities and classrooms*. Cambridge: Cambridge University Press.

Heath, S. B. (1990). The fourth vision: Literate language at work. In A. A. Lunsford, H. Moglen & J. Slevin, (Eds.), *The right to literacy* (pp. 288–306). New York: Modern Language Association of America.

Holzman, M. (1988). A post-Freirean model for adult literacy education. *College English, 50*(2), 177–189.

Hoover, J. E. (1958). *Masters of deceit*. New York: Random House.

Houston, R. (1987). The literacy campaign in Scotland, 1560–1803. In R. F. Arnove & H. J. Graff (Eds.), *National literacy campaigns: Historical and comparative perspectives* (pp. 49–64). New York: Plenum Press.

Hull, G. (1991). *Examining the relations of literacy to vocational education and work: An ethnography of a vocational program in banking and finance*. Berkeley: University of California, Graduate Department of Education.

Hull, G., Rose, M., Fraser, K. L. & Castellano, M. (1991). Remediation as social construct: Perspectives from an analysis of classroom discourse. *College Composition and Communication, 42*(3), 299–329.

Hunter, D. M., & Babcock, C. G. (1967). Some aspects of the intrapsychic structure of certain American Negroes as viewed in the intercultural dynamic. *The Psychoanalytic Study of Society, 4*, 157–173.

Johansson, E. (1981). The history of literacy in Sweden. In H. Graff (Ed.), *Literacy and social development in the west: A reader* (pp. 65–98). Cambridge: Cambridge University Press.

Johnston, W. B., & Packer, A. E. (1987). *Workforce 2000: Work and workers for the 21st century*. Washington, DC: Hudson Institute.

Jordan, J. (1990). Nobody mean more to me than you and the future life of Willie Jordan. In P. C. Hay, E. H. Schor, & R. DiYanni (Eds.), *Women's voices: Visions and perspectives* (pp. 107–118). New York: McGraw-Hill.

Kazemek, F. E. (1988). Necessary changes: Professional involvement in adult literacy programs. *Harvard Educational Review, 58*(4), 464–487.

Lave, J. (1988). *Cognition in practice: Mind, mathematics, and culture in everyday life*. New York: Cambridge University Press.

Leslie, V. K. A. (1988). A myth of the southern lady: Antebellum proslavery rhetoric and the proper place of woman. In C. Dillman (Ed.), *Southern women* (pp. 19–33). New York: Hemisphere Publishing.

Leslie, V. K. A. (1990). *Woman of color, daughter of privilege: Amanda America Dixon 1849–1893.* Unpublished doctoral dissertation, Emory University, Atlanta.

Lewis, M. A. (1967). Slavery and personality: A further comment. *American Quarterly, 19*(1), 114–121.

Lipka, J. (1991). Toward a culturally based pedagogy: A case study of one Yup'ik Eskimo teacher. *Anthropology & Education Quarterly, 22*(3), 203–223.

Lockridge, K. A. (1974). *Literacy in colonial New England.* New York: W. W. Norton.

Mishel, L., & Teixeira, R. A. (1991, Fall). The myth of the coming labor shortage. *American Prospect,* pp. 98–103.

Moffet, J. (1985). Hidden impediments to improving English teaching. *Phi Delta Kappan, 67*(1), 50–56.

Mullis, I. V. S., Owen, E. H., & Phillips, G. W. (1990). *Accelerating academic achievement: A summary of findings from 20 years of the National Assessment of Educational Progress.* Princeton, NJ: Educational Testing Service.

National Center on Education and the Economy. (1990). *America's choice: High skills or low wages!* Rochester, NY: Author.

North, S. (1987). *The making of knowledge in composition: Portrait of an emerging field.* Upper Montclair, NJ: Boynton/Cook.

Office of Technology Assessment. (1990). *Worker training: Competing in the new international economy* (OTA publication no. ITE-457). Washington, DC: U.S. Government Printing Office.

Ogbu, J., & Matute-Bianchi, M. E. (1986). Understanding socio-cultural factors: Knowledge, identity, and school adjustment. In Bilingual Education Office, California State Department of Education (Ed.), *Beyond language: Social and cultural factors in schooling language minority students* (pp. 73–142). Los Angeles: Evaluation, Dissemination & Assessment Center, California State University.

Otto, W. (1991). *How to make an American quilt.* New York: Ballantine Books.

Pendered, D. (1991, September 2). The debate rages: What's the best way to teach reading. *The Atlanta Journal and Constitution,* p. A-7.

Phillipi, J. W. (1988). Matching literacy to job training: Some applications from military programs. *Journal of Reading, 31*(7), 658–666.

Phillippi, J. W. (1991). *Literacy at work: The workbook for program developers.* Westwood, NJ: Simon & Schuster.

Quigley, B. A. (1991). Exception and reward: The history and social policy development of the GED in the USA and Canada. *Adult Basic Education, 1*(1), 33.

Rachleff, P. (1991, September 2). Crisis hits work force. *The Atlanta Journal and Constution,* p. A-12.

Resnick, D. P., & Resnick, L. B. (1977). The nature of literacy: An historical exploration. *Harvard Educational Review, 47*(3), 370–385.

Rose, M. (1989). *Lives on the boundary.* New York: Free Press.

Sachs, P. (1991, November). *Thinking through technology.* Paper presented at Roundtable: Literacy and Work, sponsored by the National Center on Adult Literacy and the Northwest Regional Educational Laboratory, Portland, OR.

Sarmiento, A. R., & Kay, A. (1990). *Worker centered learning: A union guide to workplace literacy.* Washington, DC: AFL/CIO Human Resources Department.

Scott, A. F. (1970). *The southern lady from pedestal to politics.* Chicago: University of Chicago Press.

Scribner, S., & Cole, M. (1981). *The psychology of literacy.* Cambridge, MA: Harvard University Press.

Scribner, S., & Sachs, P. (1990). *A study of on-the-job training* (Technical paper No. 13). New York: Teachers College, Columbia University, National Center on Education and Employment.

Soifer, R., Irwin, M. E., Crumrine, B. M., Honzaki, E., Simmons, B. K., & Young, D. (1990). *The complete theory-to-practice handbook of adult literacy: Curriculum design and instruction.* New York: Teachers College Press.

Staff. (1989, September 25). The next challenge: Building human capital. *Business Week,* p. 242.

Steady, F. C. (1987). African feminism: A world-wide perspective. In R. Terborg-Penn, S. Harley & A. Rushing (Eds.), *Women in Africa and the African diaspora* (pp. 3–24). Washington, DC: Howard University Press.

Stein, S., & Sperazi, L. (1991, October). *Workplace education and the transformation of the workplace.* Paper presented at the American Association of Adult and Continuing Educators' annual conference, Montreal, Canada.

Stevens, E. (1987). The anatomy of mass literacy in 19th century United States. In R. F. Arnove & H. J. Graff (Eds.), *National literacy campaigns: Historical and comparative perspectives* (pp. 99–122). New York: Plenum Press.

Stimpson, C. R. (1991, November-December). Meno's boy: Hearing his story and his sister's. *Academe,* pp. 25–31.

Sticht, T. G., Armstrong, W. B., Hickey, D. T., & Caylor, J. S. (1987). *Cast off youth: Policy and training methods from the military experience.* New York: Praeger.

Stone, N. (1991, March-April). Does business have any business in education? *Harvard Business Review,* pp. 46–62.

Strickland, S. (1990). Confrontational pedagogy and traditional literacy studies. *College English, 52*(3), 291–300.

Terborg-Penn, R. (1987). Women in the African diaspora: An overview of an interdisciplinary research conference. In R. Terborg-Penn, S. Harley & A. Rushing (Eds.), *Women in Africa and the African diaspora* (pp. 43–64). Washington, DC: Howard University Press.

Upgrading basic skills for the workplace. (1989). University Park, PA: Institute for the Study of Adult Literacy.

Walker, A. (1982). *The color purple.* New York: Washington Square Press.

Walters, K. (1990). Language, logic, and literacy. In A. A. Lunsford, H. Moglen & J. Slevin (Eds.), *The right to literacy* (pp. 173–188). New York: Modern Language Association.

Whyte, W. F. (1991). *Social theory for action: How individuals and organizations learn to change*. Newbury Park, CA: Sage Publications.

Wilcox, K. (1982). Differential socialization in the classroom: Implications for equal opportunity. In G. Spindler (Ed.), *Doing the ethnography of schooling: Educational anthropology in action* (pp. 270–308). New York: CBS College Publishing.

Zuckerman, M. B. (1989, June 12). The illiteracy epidemic. *U.S. World and News Report*, p. 72.

Index

About the Author

Sheryl Greenwood Gowen is the Assistant Director of the Center for the Study of Adult Literacy at Georgia State University, where she also teaches in the Department of Anthropology and the Division of Developmental Studies. She earned her B.A. in philosophy from Queens College, her M.Ed. from Goucher College, and her Ph.D. in curriculum and instruction from Georgia State University. Prior to her work at Georgia State, she was a classroom teacher in Saudi Arabia, Maryland, Florida, and Georgia. In 1991, she was a finalist for the National Council of Teachers of English Outstanding Researcher Award.